Walking with God

Books by William C. Mills

Pastoral Ministry

*Church, World, and Kingdom: The Eucharistic Foundations
of Alexander Schmemann's Pastoral Theology*

Kyprian Kern: Orthodox Pastoral Service

*Called to Serve: Readings on Ministry From the Orthodox
Church*

Church and World: Essays in Honor of Michael Plekon

Biblical Prayer and Spirituality

A 30 Day Retreat: A Personal Guide to Spiritual Renewal

Walking with God: Stories of Life and Faith

Come Follow Me

The Prayer of St. Ephrem: A Biblical Commentary

Our Father: A Prayer for Christian Living

Encountering Jesus in the Gospels

Lectionary Series

A Light to the Gentiles: Reflections on the Gospel of Luke

*Baptize All Nations: Reflections on the Gospel of Matthew for
the Pentecostal Season*

Feasts of Faith: Reflections on the Major Feast Days

From Pascha to Pentecost: Reflections on the Gospel of John

*Let Us Atend: Reflections on the Gospel of Mark for the
Lenten Season*

*Prepare O Bethlehem: Reflections on the Scripture Readings
for the Christmas-Epiphany Season*

WALKING WITH GOD

Stories of Life and Faith

William C. Mills

First Published by Orthodox Research Institute, 2014
Reprinted by OCABS Press, 2016

© 2014 William C. Mills

Cover photo: Walters Ms. W.592, Gospels. fol. 192b. Jesus' entry into Jerusalem.

ISBN: 1-60191-036-3 (Paperback)

TABLE OF CONTENTS

INTRODUCTION

As a pastor and as a teacher of courses in Bible and Spirituality, I find that most people want to learn more about Jesus and are seeking an authentic Christian faith but are tired of pleasant platitudes or dry dogmatic formulas that are often heard in Sunday sermons: "If you give ten percent of your income to the Church, God will bless you" or "Just pray and you will be okay" or even worse, a long list of dos and don'ts! People see through these trite messages. They come to church for inspiration and healing, and they leave hungry. They want God to help transform their lives. It is not enough to memorize a list of rules and regulations or even to memorize a collection of scriptural passages. People want to know more about the Bible and how they can live a better life. Even children don't like to memorize math or spelling rules, they want to see how math works, how formulas are put together and how they can be applied in daily living. The same pertains to the Scriptures. But what to do?

While people may not memorize particular scriptural passages or facts about Jesus, everyone likes a good story. There is nothing better than cuddling up on a cold winter night with a cup of hot tea or cocoa and your favorite book.

Children especially love stories. As soon as the teacher announces that it's story time, they race to the carpet and eagerly wait for the story to begin. They sit in a circle with their eyes wide open, mesmerized with princes and princesses, witches and warlocks, wars and weddings, and of course, dragons and adventure. When I was a child, I remember walking to the library with my mother. It was only a five-block walk, but we couldn't get to the library fast enough. We sat there together with other moms and children listening to the librarian read story after story. During those weekly reading programs, I was transported to different worlds, worlds where animals talked or where people could fly. I envisioned a world where children ruled and where we could eat chocolate all day and not get sick. Children know a good story when they hear one, which is why the Harry Potter series continues to be so popular.

Stories convey not just information but also help form our faith. A friend of mine told me a story about growing up in Palestine during the British Mandate period. The family was very poor. Her mom stayed home with her brothers and sisters while her father went to work. One day after work, her father stopped on his way home and bought something for the family. When he got home, he told his family that he had a surprise for them. He searched through his satchel and put down a shiny red apple on the table.

He looked over to his wife and said, "I think you should have it." She thought for a minute and said, "No, I think the youngest should have it. She is very sickly. She needs the nourishment." My friend's sister, the youngest, said, "No, I think daddy should have it. He works so hard every day, bringing home money to help the family." Then the middle child shouted out, "Maybe daddy can divide the apple into five pieces and we can all taste it." The father and mother looked at each other and smiled. The mother cut the apple into five equal pieces. This story, my friend told me, carried her through some very hard times. She eventually left Palestine and came to America, working as the first female physician in a hospital in Spartanburg, SC. I share this apple story with you as an example of the power of stories, but at the same time, now her story becomes your story too. You are free to pass this story on to your friends and family and in that way it will live on in the minds and hearts of others.

Jesus devoted His entire ministry to telling stories. We call them parables. These parables reveal the deep meaning of forgiveness, as in the parable of the Prodigal Son, judgment, as we hear in the Parable of the Talents. Jesus traveled around Galilee telling stories of love, forgiveness, repentance, and community life. He also taught through His example, healing the sick and the suffering with a the touch of His hand or a simple command like, "Go and wash and be clean." Jesus was smart too. He used everyday common images to help spread the Good News: shepherds, planting, harvesting, yeast, light, trees and shrubs. When Jesus spoke, everyone could understand. Eventually these stories were written down and collected in four gospels: Matthew, Mark, Luke, and John. Every Sunday we hear a different gospel lesson as a way to learn not just what Jesus did and said but what His words mean for daily living. The gospel contains life-giving words, words that encourage, inspire, reprove, explain, and inform. Each Sunday when we hear stories about Jesus we are being formed and shaped as His disciples.

Walking With God: Stories of Life and Faith are pastoral and practical stories collected throughout the years. As a father, husband, pastor, and teacher, I have both heard and told hundreds of stories. The stories included in *Walking With God* are stories of struggling with what it means to live a Godly life.

Each chapter includes a "Food for Thought" section with a few follow-up reflections for the reader to consider. I have also included some additional scriptural passages for the reader to read on their own. I hope that *Walking With God* becomes a regular resource for prayer, Scripture study, and continuing conversation about living a holy life in Christ. May these stories help you with your walk of faith.

CHAPTER ONE

CARING AND COMPASSION

When He entered Capernaum, a centurion came to Him, appealing to Him and saying, "Lord, my servant is lying at home paralyzed, in terrible distress." And He said to him, "I will come and cure him." The centurion answered, "Lord, I am not worthy to have You come under my roof; but only speak the word, and my servant will be healed." (Matthew 8:5–8)

Two sayings have remained with me throughout my life: "you don't know someone until you walk in their shoes" and "the best training is on-the-job training."

Our college professors tell us that they can only teach us basic theories and methods. They tell us that after graduation, we will enter the real world and learn the rest. They remind us that a college education is limited; we would need to be life-long learners.

The same advice can be applied to parenting. One of my good friends once joked, "If God wanted us to have a parenting manual, He would have given us one!" He's right. The best way to learn about parenting is to be a parent: changing diapers, helping with homework, waiting in carpool, and attending basketball and soccer games. You learn parenting when you act as a parent.

Walking in someone else's shoes is supposed to make us more compassionate, more caring, and more sympathetic. When you have sympathy for someone you feel for them, you sit with them in their pain and their joys. You cannot show sympathy for someone until you walk with them during times of crisis and pain.

Matthew tells us that one day Jesus visited Capernaum, a small village on the eastern shore of the Sea of Galilee. The name Capernaum means, "the house of comfort." While in Capernaum, Jesus encountered a Roman centurion. A centurion was a high-ranking military officer in the Roman army. You might be asking yourself, so what? Jesus healed a lot of people, right? Yes, Jesus did heal a lot of people, but it was not customary for Jewish rabbis to visit Roman households. Most Jews during that time considered the Romans the enemy and when Jesus was seen speaking with this Roman soldier, the villagers would assume that Jesus was a traitor. Talk about being countercultural! By going to Capernaum, Jesus stretched our limits of love and compassion. It's easy to love those around us: our family, friends, our next-door neighbors, or those from our culture or religion. By going to Capernaum, Jesus forced us out of our comfort zone.

Throughout the gospel stories, Jesus stretches our ideas of love and compassion. He goes out of His way and speaks with a Samaritan woman. He eats with the Pharisees and Sadducees. He calls tax collectors like Matthew and Zachaeus. Jesus reaches out to the poor, to the orphan, to the widow, and to the outcast, to all of those whom society has forgotten. The prophets in the Old Testament constantly remind us of this:

*He has told you, O mortal, what is good; and what does the Lord require of you but to do **justice, and to love kindness, and to walk humbly with your God?*** (Micah 6:8)

*Hear this word, you cows of Bashan who are on Mount Samaria, **who oppress the poor, who crush the needy, who say to their husbands, "Bring something to drink!"** The Lord God has sworn by his holiness: The time is surely coming upon you, when they shall take you away with hooks, even the last of you with fishhooks. Through breaches in the wall you shall leave, each one straight ahead; and you shall be flung out into Harmon, says the Lord.* (Amos 4:1–3)

Ah, you who make iniquitous decrees, who write oppressive statutes, to turn aside the needy from justice and to rob the poor of my people of their right, that widows may be your spoil, and that you may make the orphans your prey! What will you do on the day of punishment, in the calamity that will come from far away? To whom will you flee for help, and where will you leave your wealth, so as not to crouch among the prisoners or fall among the slain? For all this his anger has not turned away; his hand is stretched out still. (Isaiah 10:1-4)

Amos, Micah, and Isaiah are very clear. God is not happy when we neglect empathy for the least and the lowest among us. We erect walls and fences. We care only for people within these safe boundaries, yet God is interested in people outside of these boundaries too. A long time ago a priest friend of mine told me that he wanted to start an outreach program in his parish, a food bank for the local community. After he created an outline and details for the program he presented his ideas to the parish council. After reviewing the plans they said, "But Father, we don't want those people hanging around our parish!" My friend was saddened at hearing their response and the parish never started the food bank. Unfortunately, this type of negative response is not uncommon in parish life.

We feel uncomfortable around people from different ethnic, racial, social, or financial backgrounds. It is very easy to withdraw and circle the wagons. We keep people out.

Yet Matthew reminds us that Jesus raised the bar for discipleship. He challenged us to stretch our love and compassion. The odd thing though is that the more we love and the more we care, the more we realize we can love and care.

Food for Thought

1. Think of a time when you could have helped someone but didn't. How did you feel afterwards when you realized you had lost a good opportunity to show love and compassion?

2. Have you been in a time of need and someone helped you? What were the specific circumstances? How did it make you feel afterwards?

3. Read: Matthew 5:1–20, John 10:1–18, 2 Corinthians 1:3–14.

CHAPTER TWO

CRAZIES AND CRACKPOTS

When He came to the other side, to the country of the Gadarenes, two demoniacs coming out of the tombs met Him. They were so fierce that no one could pass that way. Suddenly they shouted, "What have You to do with us, Son of God? Have You come here to torment us before the time?" (Mathew 8:28–30)

When driving through town, I often see a man walking up and down Main Street. His hair is unwashed. He has one pant leg up and one pant leg down. His socks do not match. He dresses like this all year long; winter, spring, summer, and fall: no jacket, no gloves, no scarf, no hat, no shorts or sneakers, just a dirty pair of jeans and a t-shirt. After seeing him like this for a while I became curious. Who was he?

I made a mental note to ask my barber who knows everyone in town. Joe has lived in town his entire life, so I knew that Joe could answer my questions. The next time I went for a haircut I started asking Joe about the stranger. He interrupted me with a smile on his face, "Oh, you mean Richard!" Apparently Richard was born with severe autism and, therefore, never could hold down a job. He dropped out of high school, and his parents died when he was young. He lives on the edge of town in a modest one-bedroom apartment. Someone checks on him a few days a week.

Then there is Mary Ann. Mary Ann is a woman in her mid-fifties. If you saw Mary Ann walking on the street, you would think she was an executive. Her hair is perfect, her clothes are trendy, and she always wears beautiful jewelry and carries a matching handbag. If you meet her, she may say, "I know you are but what am I?" Or sometimes she will mimic someone if they ask her, "Mary Ann, it's a lovely day isn't it?" She will repeat, "Lovely day isn't it?" This is normal behavior for a five- or six-year-old, but not for a fifty-five-year-old woman.

Mary Ann suffers from MPD, otherwise known as multiple personality disorder. Mary Ann has about five different personalities. Sometimes she acts like a five-year-old; sometimes she is a college-age person. She will suffer like this for the rest of her life. Pills and medication help but will not heal her.

During Jesus' lifetime, people like Mary Ann and Richard would have been treated like the two men in the gospel and chained to tombs or caves, sent off to the edge of town. They would have been drowned, stoned, beaten, or exiled, sent away to live a life of wandering and begging. People like this were stigmatized, labeled as crazies or crackpots. Even today most people will avoid a Richard or Mary Ann, keeping them at arm's length. Since Richard and Mary Ann do not fit our common cultural notion of normal, we can't deal with them. We treat them as pariahs.

Yet what did Jesus do? Did Jesus avoid these people? Did He ignore their need for wholeness and healing? No, He went out of His way to help them. When Jesus encountered these men in the tombs, He could have avoided them, walked around the area, or walked away. Yet Jesus went directly to the village and reached out and healed these men from their demonic possession. Jesus challenged every religious and cultural custom which taught that anyone with a mental or physical sickness was bad one and in order to keep oneself clean, one had to keep them away, keep them in tombs, cemeteries, outside the city walls. Jesus broke those social customs and reached out and healed. He drove those demons out into the sea.

We live in the Twenty-first century and forget that demons are still with us today. These demons are not little evil men walking around in red suits but they certainly are around. The demon of jealousy is a big one. This is the little voice in your ear telling you that you don't have enough of everything. You need more. You deserve more. If your neighbor buys a new car, you need a new car. I suffered from this demon when I was a teenager. My friend had an Atari video game. I used to go over to his house and play with it. All I wanted from my parents was an Atari video game, but my parents never bought me one. I was jealous of my friend for a very long time.

Then there is the demon of negativity. This demon says, "I'm not a good person." Now we all mess up and hurt other people, but according to Genesis, God created everything and created it good. Yes, Adam and Eve disobeyed God, but at the root or foundation of everything, they were created for good. We grow up and think not that we do bad things from time to time but that *we* are bad, that we are broken from the beginning. This is really stinking thinking. If we think that we are bad, then we aren't living a full life, we are not using our gifts, talents and resources for the spreading of the good news.

Jesus comes to us today, just as He came to those two men in Gergassa. He reaches out His healing hand to us. Are we going to take it? Are we going to begin our walk on the path to healing and wholeness, a path that leads to life or are we going to stay chained up in those deep dark caves where we are stigmatized and isolated? No one is going to make us reach out and grab that hand. No one is going to make us seek out that divine healing. We have to choose it for ourselves, to choose that narrow path that leads to life.

FOOD FOR THOUGHT

1. Take a few moments and think about the demons in your life. Can you drive them out? This is not easy to do but you will not find healing and wholeness unless you claim power over the things that get between you and God.

2. It is customary for parishioners to participate in the Sacrament of Confession. Confession is a way that we name and claim all of the demons that drag us down. You are encouraged to confess your sins to God and get back on the narrow path of salvation.

3. Read: Matthew 12:22–29, Mark 9:14–29, Luke 4:1–13.

CHAPTER THREE

MEETING GOD

When the time came for their purification according to the law of Moses, they brought him up to Jerusalem to present him to the Lord (as it is written in the law of the Lord, "Every firstborn male shall be designated as holy to the Lord"), and they offered a sacrifice according to what is stated in the law of the Lord, "a pair of turtledoves or two young pigeons." Now there was a man in Jerusalem whose name was Simeon; this man was righteous and devout, looking forward to the consolation of Israel, and the Holy Spirit rested on him. (Luke 2:22–25)

When I first started parish ministry, I was afraid of visiting parishioners. I always had sweaty palms and my heart would beat faster as I approached the driveway. Crazy thoughts ran through my head. I was worried about what they might think of me. I worried about what we'd talk about. I was worried that they might be angry at God. I never knew what to expect. Would they ask me questions that I couldn't answer? Most of the time, my fears were for nothing, because most people were cordial and hospitable. I was worked up about nothing.

Luke tells us that after Jesus was born, Mary and Joseph brought Jesus to the Jerusalem Temple along with two pigeons for the offering. We do not know who Simeon was other than what Luke tells us: a righteous man waiting for the consolation of Israel. Simeon was not alone. Later in the passage we hear about another person, a woman named Anna, who was also in the Temple, "And there was a prophetess Anna, the daughter of Phanuel, of the tribe of Asher; she was a great age, having lived with her husband seven years from her virginity, and as a widow till she was eighty-four" (Luke 2:36–37).

Simeon and Anna waited in the Temple. They waited for a messiah. They heard the prophecies from Isaiah, Jeremiah, and Ezekiel about the messiah. They knew that one day God would send a savior. Simeon was probably wondering, "Will the messiah come to-day?" He was hoping and expecting, like a little girl waiting by the window for her daddy to come home. Every day Simeon and Anna waited, and they waited, and they waited, but no messiah. Then Luke tells us that one day, Mary and Joseph brought the baby Jesus to be dedicated to the Lord as was the Jewish custom. Finally, the messiah arrived. Simeon was so excited that he broke out in song:

> *"Master, now you are dismissing your servant in peace, according to your word; for my eyes have seen your salvation, which you have prepared in the presence of all peoples, a light for revelation to the Gentiles and for glory to your people Israel." And the child's father and mother were amazed at what was being said about Him. Then Simeon blessed them and said to His mother Mary, "This child is destined for the falling and the rising of many in Israel, and to be a sign that will be opposed so that the inner thoughts of many will be revealed — and a sword will pierce your own soul too."* (Luke 2:29–35)

Simeon and Anna encountered not just any baby that day; they encountered the messiah, the Christ child. Their lives were changed forever. Actually everyone's lives were changed as we read in the Gospel of John, "And the Word became flesh and dwelt among us, full of grace and truth; we have beheld his glory, glory as the only Son of the Father" (John 1:14).

I heard a story of a pastor who had a large parish in Chicago. One of his parishioners, Sarah asked him if he would visit her friend Maria, who was dying. The pastor, however, was not interested in traveling across town to visit a person whom he had never met and who wasn't a member of his congregation. After thinking about it for a few moments, though he decided to go. It was quite a journey too. Since he lived in the suburbs, he had to drive through rush hour traffic. After a forty-five minute drive through downtown Chicago, the pastor eventually found her apartment. After opening the door to the building, he noticed that there was no elevator. Maria lived on the fifth floor. So he walked up the five flights of steps. He knocked on the door and a neighbor friend was already there, "Hello," he said to the neighbor, "My name is Pastor Michael and I'm from All Souls Church, Maria's friend asked me to visit." Pastor Michael didn't know what to expect, especially from a dying woman. His experience with the dying was mixed. Some people are mad at God, others are scared, and some are indifferent.

He walked back into Maria's bedroom and saw a waif of a woman, her eyes sunken in and her cheekbones pronounced. He could see her bones through her nightgown. She could barely speak, but she motioned for Pastor Michael to sit down. He sat down and explained who he was and Maria smiled. She said she wanted to tell him something, so Pastor Michael bent down and she told him about her two failed marriages, the anger she felt towards several friends, and the fact that she and her son were not reconciled. She also told him that she believed in Jesus but she was never baptized. Pastor Michael said a few words to her and then without being pushy he said, "Maria, I know that you believe in Jesus but don't go to Church and all but I was wondering if you would want to be baptized." She responded quickly, "Yes, father, I would like that." So Pastor Michael took out some holy water, said a few brief prayers and sprinkled holy water on her head and then anointed her with holy oil, "The grace of the Holy Spirit be with you Maria, now and always." Maria smiled and her eyes closed. She was tired. Pastor Michael said goodbye to the neighbor and drove back home.

When Pastor Michael returned home, he immediately called Sarah. He told her about the long drive, about the meeting with Maria and then said, "You know, Sarah, someone else was there the other day. God was there too." He went on and told Sarah that it was the first time in his ministry that he had felt a deep sense of God's presence.

We encounter God in a variety of ways and in many places, most of which are not in Church. Every Sunday we go to church and expect God to show up, and He often does, but the Scriptures show us that God reveals Himself in a lot of other places too. He revealed Himself to Abraham in the middle of the desert, He appeared to Jacob in a dream, He knocked the Apostle Paul off his horse on the way to Damascus, and He appeared to Mary Magdalene in the garden on the first Easter morning. God is like that, He comes and goes as He chooses and many times it is not where we expect Him to be. However, when we encounter God, it is a holy moment, a moment of love and peace, but also a moment of repentance, because we know how far we have wandered away from Him.

FOOD FOR THOUGHT

1. Take some time and think about your life. Like Simeon and Anna, have you ever felt God's deep presence in your life? What did it feel like? How did you respond?

2. Many people in the New Testament are surprised when they encounter Jesus: Mary Magdalene, Nathaniel, Cleopas, Thomas, the Apostle Paul. God surprises a lot of people in a variety of places. Has God ever surprised you?

3. Read: John 1:35–51, 20:11–18, Acts 9:10–22.

CHAPTER FOUR

COMPLAIN, COMPLAIN, COMPLAIN

Then Jesus said, "There was a man who had two sons. The younger of them said to his father, 'Father, give me the share of the property that will belong to me.' So he divided his property between them. A few days later the younger son gathered all he had and traveled to a distant country, and there he squandered his property in dissolute living. When he had spent everything, a severe famine took place throughout that country, and he began to be in need. So he went and hired himself out to one of the citizens of that country, who sent him to his fields to feed the pigs." (Luke 15:11–15)

One summer our family went on our summer vacation and we visited another church. It wasn't just beautiful, it was gorgeous! The sidewalk was made with hand laid tumbled brick which was very inviting. The inside of the church building had a forty or fifty foot domed ceiling with archways along the sides with plenty of natural sunlight coming down from above the high windows in the domed area. The floor was nailed down wide plank wooden floors. The front doors were solid oak with matching cast iron hinges and locks. The entire church building looked amazing.

While walking through this church, I started comparing my own church to this one. They had a brick sidewalk and we had a plain cement one. They had a dome in the center of the ceiling and we didn't. They had oak doors and we had regular ones.

We often compare ourselves with other people; our families with other families, our jobs with other jobs, our house with other houses. We focus on what we don't have rather than being grateful for what we do have. We sound like the older brother in this gospel lesson. We go through life complaining!

Luke tells us that this man has two sons, one asks for his inheritance and leaves, spending it on loose living, squandering what he has just been given. The older son stays with the father and maintains his usual life. Yet who complains the most when the younger son returns home? The older brother! Granted, the younger son made serious mistakes and squandered his money, but he did eventually return home. All the while his older brother had a warm bed to sleep in, three hot meals a day. He had his parents, his family, and his work. He had safety and security and comfort. He was doing great and, guess what, he still was not happy! Sounds like a whiny teenager, doesn't he?

We shouldn't be surprised at the older boy's reaction. Complaining is very biblical. We see it right in the beginning of the Old Testament. In the Book of Exodus, the Israelites are in bondage and slavery, it's hot, it's sandy, and they're tired. They beg Moses to do something, so Moses asks God and God leads them out of slavery. Moses takes the Israelites across the Red Sea and brings them to the Promised Land. Just a few weeks into the trip and they sound like most teenagers. They tell Moses that they're hungry. Moses goes back to Yahweh with their complaints and what does Yahweh do: He gives them manna. Now they're happy. So they eat their fill of manna. But guess what, they still are not happy. They murmur against God. Even while the food from heaven was in their mouth they yelled at God. Now the problem was that they were thirsty. It's very hot in the desert, and there's not much water around. So they complain to Moses. Moses strikes a big rock with his staff and out comes fresh water. This same story is played out again and again in the Old Testament; those Israelites are never happy, they complain too much. The Israelites focused so much on their hunger and thirst that they weren't grateful for their freedom from slavery.

We murmur against God too. Every Sunday we come and partake of Jesus' Body and Blood, the bread from heaven and the water of life, yet don't we still complain and grumble and murmur against Him?

We focus so much on what we don't have and neglect to give thanks for the many blessings we do have; our parish communities, our priests and pastors, our family and friends, our jobs, our very life; it's all a gift. The fact that we can gather every Sunday and worship freely and openly is a gift, yet we still grumble. Perhaps we can turn, like the younger brother, and tell God we're sorry for everything that we do wrong, and become grateful for the many blessings that we do receive from God the Father. Luke ends by telling us that the father in the story left the door open, the lights on, a hot meal ready for his younger son (which is us) to return home. God is always waiting for us, He just wants us to make the first step.

FOOD FOR THOUGHT

1. Sometimes we can identify with the younger son and other times we can identify with the older son. Once in a while you might feel like the father. Take some time to look at your life. Right now, which of the three main people in the gospel story do you most identify with? Why?

2. God gives us so many talents and treasures yet so often we waste them. We don't use them. We're not grateful. Take a moment of quiet time and thank God for the many blessings that you have. Give thanks for both the small and big things in life.

3. Read: Matthew 5:40–45, 25:14–30, and John 17.

CHAPTER FIVE

CARRYING OUR CROSS

He called the crowd with His disciples, and said to them, "If any want to become My followers, let them deny themselves and take up their cross and follow Me. For those who want to save their life will lose it, and those who lose their life for My sake, and for the sake of the gospel, will save it. For what will it profit them to gain the whole world and forfeit their life? Indeed, what can they give in return for their life? (Mark 8:34–37)

When I was studying at seminary, we had our classes, church services, and our work assignments. All of the fulltime students had some type of volunteer work, whether it was answering the phones, sorting the mail, cutting the grass, or shelving books in the library. For two years, I served as the lunch crew captain. Every day at 1:00 PM, four of us left class early and walked down to the seminary refectory and served lunch. After the thanksgiving prayer, we had to clean up and wash the dishes.

But the job that no one wanted, the job that everyone dreaded, was sacristan. What is a sacristan you say? The sacristan was responsible for lighting all the candles, bringing up the vestments from the basement storage area, and making sure there was enough wine, bread, charcoal, and incense for the services. The sacristan was also required to arrive early for the services, which meant 7:00 AM for Matins, 5:00 PM for Vespers. During Lent, there was compline at 9:00 PM, so the sacristan had to be at church by 8:30 PM.

For my third year, I was hoping for an easy job, maybe a job in the mail room, or cutting grass on the grounds crew, or answering phones in the main office. So on the first day of school I ran up to the second floor of the main building where my mailbox was located and found a plain white envelope with my name on it. I quickly opened the letter and there was a short typed letter from the Dean of Students: William Mills, Sacristan. I was livid. So many thoughts raced through my head. Didn't they know that I was a third year seminarian and I wanted an easy job? Didn't they realize that I was going to be ordained soon? Didn't they know that I had books to read and papers to write? How dare they! No way was I going to be the sacristan!

The next day I made an appointment with the Dean of Students. Before the meeting, I mentally prepared a short response to the letter, I wanted to have all of my information ready. I took at seat in his office he said, "You know Bill, I am so glad that you're going to be the sacristan this year. You are such a dedicated student, responsible, caring, kind, nice." He had a big smile on his face too. Clearly he was proud of me. He knew I could do a good job since I had done very well on the lunch crew. He also had been a priest for over thirty years and was no dummy; he must have seen the white envelope sticking out from my pants pocket. I sat in my chair speechless. After hearing all of those compliments about me, how could I argue with him?

I was a slow learner, but I soon realized that after a while, being a sacristan wasn't that bad. After all I knew that I had to be in chapel anyway. It was quiet. I could think and have a lot of quiet time just to sit and reflect on my life and my future as a priest. Being a sacristan wasn't that difficult. The guys on the grounds crew had to shovel snow in bitter cold temperature and cut grass and rake leaves when it was cold and damp outside. The poor guys on the lunch and dinner crews had dirty dishes to wash and the students in the library had piles of books to shelve.

I learned that after you accept it, you realize that the load is easier to carry.

So many people in this world suffer so much: physically, spiritually, emotionally, and psychologically. There comes a time, however, when our pain might not go away, it might be with us forever. Here I think of so many elderly people who suffer excruciating pain yet manage to keep going, not letting the pain get in the way of their living, or those suffering from many types of addictions, or from other terrible situations.

Jesus certainly suffered during His life. He carried His cross. Just before He died, before His trial and crucifixion, Jesus and His disciples went into the Garden of Gethsemane to pray. Three times Jesus asked the Lord to take His cup of suffering away from Him, but He ended the prayer with, "Not as I will, but as Thou wilt," which is similar to the phrase that we find in the Lord's Prayer, "Thy will be done on earth as it is in heaven." Not Jesus' will but God the Father's will. The Apostle Paul says the same thing slightly differently. In 1 Corinthians, he prays to God asking that the mysterious "thorn in his flesh" whatever it was, be taken from him. Some scholars think that Paul was short and people laughed at him, others think he was like Moses and had a stuttering problem, but three times he prayed to God the Father that this thorn be taken from him and three times God says, "My power is made perfect in weakness." Perfection through weakness, now that's countercultural! Jesus was weak. Jesus takes our weakness and crucifies it with Him on the cross; He takes on all of our pain and suffering and trials and tribulations and crucifies them with Himself. And we participate in that crucifixion. Paul says that it is not I who lives but Christ who lives in me.

Ultimately, however, the cross is not so much a burden as it is a cross of love and service. Jesus did not take the cross for Himself, that would have been egotistical and selfish. He takes the cross on for us and for the life of the world and its salvation. We participate in that cross in our service to others. Just before Jesus goes to Gethsemane, His last teaching, His last ministerial act with His disciples is that He takes off His shirt, takes a bowl of water and starts washing Peter's feet. Peter, of course, cannot believe this; he balks and says, "No Lord, you cannot do this. You are our rabbi, you are the messiah." But Jesus keeps at it and says, Peter, if you don't let Me wash you, you cannot be part of My family, you cannot be part of my community. Peter then says, "Okay Lord, not just my feet, but my hands and my head too." In other words, if you want to follow Me you also have to wash feet. And Peter and the other disciples do. They wash the feet of everyone.

FOOD FOR THOUGHT

1. What are the things that cause you suffering right now? If you are not currently suffering what are the things that you suffered from before?

2. Discipleship requires that each of us carry our cross daily. Are you having a hard time carrying your cross? Remember that we do not walk alone. God is with us too.

3. Read: Psalm 23, Mark 6:31–38, Galatians 2:17–21.

CHAPTER SIX

HIGH ANXIETY

Therefore I tell you, do not worry about your life, what you will eat or what you will drink, or about your body, what you will wear. Is not life more than food, and the body more than clothing? Look at the birds of the air; they neither sow nor reap nor gather into barns, and yet your heavenly Father feeds them. Are you not of more value than they? And can any of you by worrying add a single hour to your span of life? And why do you worry about clothing? Consider the lilies of the field, how they grow; they neither toil nor spin, yet I tell you, even Solomon in all his glory was not clothed like one of these. But if God so clothes the grass of the field, which is alive today and tomorrow is thrown into the oven, will he not much more clothe you — you of little faith? (Matthew 6:25–30)

Some people are afraid of flying. During major holidays, like Thanksgiving and Christmas, or during the summer vacation season, more people travel, which means more people on airplanes. I always chuckle when the flight attendant closes the airplane door and says, "Please prepare for takeoff." One person starts mumbling the Lord's Prayer. Someone else makes the sign of the cross. I wonder if these people also go to church regularly or they just get religious on airplanes? It's like the saying I once heard, "There are no atheists in fox holes."

Jesus tells us not to be afraid.

A few summers ago our family vacationed in New Hampshire. We stayed in a small New England town, one of those off-the-road places with a colonial style, white clapboard church, a post office, ice cream parlor, and a cemetery. If you blinked twice, you'd miss the downtown area. My wife wanted to visit some antique shops and after asking directions from several people we eventually heard about one near main street. The store was on the other side of a river. A roaring white-capped river snaked through town dividing the town in two. As we walked along the gravel path from Main Street, the path suddenly stopped. From where we were standing, we could see the antique barn across the river with its red shingles and black metal roof. The foot bridge was nothing more than an old rickety wooden bridge about three feet wide and the wooden slats were about five or six inches apart. The bridge had two thick ropes on either side that served as handles — not exactly my idea of safety!

I found myself just standing in one spot. I looked down at the river and was afraid. What if we fall? What if the bridge breaks? While I was thinking about the possible problems, my wife and five-year-old daughter started walking across this wooden bridge. Do you think I followed them? No way! I stood there, scared out of my wits. There was a lump in my throat. Then I felt really stupid. I watched my wife walk across that footbridge and I knew in my mind that it was safe, yet I could not get myself to walk across. So I found a park bench nearby and sat on it watching the white-capped waves roll on below me as my wife and daughter walked into the antique store.

Jesus tells us do not be afraid.

Jesus prepares His disciples for ministry by teaching them several things, one of which is not to have fear. Fear is a natural emotion and Jesus knew full well that fear can be paralyzing. Fear prohibits people from moving forward, from engaging in ministry.

In the sixth chapter of Matthew, Jesus walks to the top of a mountain and begins teaching His disciples. We call this the Sermon on the Mount. The Sermon on the Mount is the core teaching of Jesus. It is where we find the Lord's Prayer, the Beatitudes, and other teachings such as fasting, prayer, almsgiving and charity. If the Sermon on the Mount is the core teaching of the Gospel, then these particular verses form the central teaching of the Sermon on the

Mount, which is "be not afraid."

Jesus knew full well the trials and tribulations, the cares and concerns, the pains and the problems that lay ahead. He knew that His disciples would worry whether or not they would be received with open arms, as well as have questions about where they were going to sleep and what they were going to eat and where they would be going and who was going to help them. After all, these were fishermen; men well versed in the finer points of sardines and fishing hooks, boats and sails, not preaching, proclamation, and miracles. Jesus was preparing His disciples to enter into the mission field. He wanted them not to get distracted from their main focus.

There is a passage in the Gospel of Mark where Jesus and His disciples are on a boat. It is night and they are crossing the Sea of Galilee,

> *On that day, when evening had come, He said to them, "Let us go across to the other side." And leaving the crowd behind, they took Him with them in the boat, just as He was. Other boats were with Him. A great windstorm arose, and the waves beat into the boat, so that the boat was already being swamped. But He was in the stern, asleep on the cushion; and they woke Him up and said to Him, "Teacher, do You not care that we are perishing?" He woke up and rebuked the wind, and said to the sea, "Peace! Be still!" Then*

the wind ceased, and there was a dead calm. He said to them, "Why are you afraid? Have you still no faith?" And they were filled with great awe and said to one another, "Who then is this, that even the wind and the sea obey Him?" (Mark 4:35–41)

The antidote against anxiety is faith. When we put our trust and faith in God, our anxieties take a back seat. When we trust God, we realize that we make mountains out of molehills and waste so many hours worrying about things that really don't matter. It's an endless cycle: we worry, then we obsess, then we worry some more. And what happens? We take our focus off God and following Him and we put the focus on ourselves. We lose our focus on the kingdom. We take our focus off of being His disciples.

FOOD FOR THOUGHT

1. Take a few moments and make a list of things that continue to cause you fear?

2. Take a few moments and make a list of all of the fears that you have overome in your life. How did you overcome them? Do you still have fears to-day? What are they? Do you think you will over-come these new fears?

3. Read: Mark 4:35–41, Luke 1:12–30, John 14:23–29.

CHAPTER SEVEN

CHANGE IS EVERYWHERE

In those days John the Baptist appeared in the wilderness of Judea, proclaiming, "Repent, for the kingdom of heaven has come near." This is the one of whom the Prophet Isaiah spoke when he said, "The voice of one crying out in the wilderness: 'Prepare the way of the Lord, make His paths straight.' Now John wore clothing of camel's hair with a leather belt around his waist, and his food was locusts and wild honey. Then the people of Jerusalem and all Judea were going out to him, and all the region along the Jordan, and they were baptized by him in the river Jordan, confessing their sins. (Matthew 3:1–6)

There are small changes in life and there are big changes in life, but one thing is certain: if you live, you will encounter change. When my wife and I lived in New York, we banked at the First Union Bank. I was thrilled to get my first checking account. They even gave me a green lollipop, along with the check-book and checks. I was officially an adult. When we relocated to North Carolina, I went online and found that they also had First Union banks in North Carolina so there was no need for me to change banks. Boy was I wrong. After a few years, Wachovia Bank, a much larger bank, bought out First Union, and now the bank was called Wachovia. So my green lollipops went from just plain green to green and blue. I got a new set of checks and new information from the bank. So now I used a Wachovia debit card and Wachovia checkbook and went to the local Wachovia branch office. Then a few years later, Wells Fargo, an even larger bank, bought out Wachovia and my bluish green lollipops changed to red and orange and I got yet another set of checks and new information from the bank. But this type of thing happens a lot. Life requires change.

Change is at the center of this gospel lesson. John the Baptist is at the Jordan River baptizing people. He tells them to repent for the kingdom of heaven is now. "Change" is what John is really saying: change for a new era has come, change for a new day has come, change the way you think about God, change the way you think about your neighbors, change the way you think about the world around you, change the way you think about money and material things, change. So everyone from around the area came and was baptized, and among those people was Jesus. And after Jesus got out of the water, His message was the same as John's and all the prophets before Him — Isaiah, Ezekiel, Amos, Jonah, Hosea — change, change, change.

Why so much concern about change? You think they would get it already. Actually not! Most of us don't want to change; change takes work. Heck, we don't want to work. We like ourselves the way we are don't we? I know I do! Change requires a lot of soul searching and inward looking and altering our lifestyle, sometimes a little and sometimes a lot. We'd rather stay with our usual ho-hum life. That is exactly what a lot of people did back then too. Matthew says that people from all the surrounding towns and villages and cities came to hear John preach. Do you think they all accepted that message and got baptized? Some did but most didn't. The first thing Jesus says after He is baptized is actually from the Prophet Isaiah, "The people who sat in the darkness have seen a great light." The new light, of course, being Jesus Himself. However, Isaiah also says that the nation of Israel is a stubborn and stiff-necked people who are hard hearted, who are selfish rather than self-less. He says that they have eyes but do not see, ears but do not hear, mouths but do not speak. In other words, they do not listen to God. The message is clear, from Isaiah, John the Baptist, and Jesus: change is necessary; it will be hard but change we must. Isaiah was talking about Israel, but He is also talking to us; we are stubborn and stiff-necked and hard hearted and have eyes but do not see, and ears but do not hear, and mouths but do not speak.

To change also means to be open to the Spirit, to go where He leads us even if it is a strange and new land. Where does the Spirit lead Jesus after His baptism? To the desert! Yes, the hot, vast, waterless, plant-less Judean desert where He is tempted by Satan! One would think it would lead Him to Galilee where it's cooler and there's plenty of vegetation. The Spirit leads Jesus to the desert to test Him.

We need to be open to the Spirit too, to go where He leads us, and it might be scary and dark and seem like we don't know where we are going, but we are called to follow: repent for the kingdom of God is at hand.

Food for Thought

1. Throughout life we go through many changes. We move. We find a new job. We get married. We have children. Are there any particular changes in your life that were very painful? Take a few moments in silence and think of these changes. Write them down. Note how you overcame these changes.

2. One word we read a lot about in the gospels is the word "repent." Repent means to change direction. Repentance requires that we change our behaviors and our bad thinking. Take some time now and think of the things in your life that need changing.

3. Read: Mark 1:14–20, John 1:9–28, Romans 6:1–11.

CHAPTER EIGHT

LIVING WITH AMBIGUITY

Then Herod secretly called for the wise men and learned from them the exact time when the star had appeared. Then he sent them to Bethlehem, saying, "Go and search diligently for the child; and when you have found Him, bring me word so that I may also go and pay Him homage." When they had heard the king, they set out; and there, ahead of them, went the star that they had seen at its rising, until it stopped over the place where the child was. When they saw that the star had stopped, they were overwhelmed with joy. On entering the house, they saw the child with Mary His mother; and they knelt down and paid Him homage. Then, opening their treasure chests, they offered Him gifts of gold, frankincense, and myrrh. And having been warned in a dream not to return to Herod, they left for their own country by another road. (Matthew 2:7–12)

There are two kinds of literature. One, which most people call pulp fiction, is easy-to-read writing that ties all the loose ends together at the end; many are thrillers, suspense novels, and mysteries. Many people don't have the time or energy to sink their teeth into a difficult book. We want to be entertained and have everything turn out right at the end: the girl gets the guy and they walk off together into the sunset.

Then there is what I call literature, writing that has stood the test of time. Pulp fiction comes and goes with the tide, one day a *New York Times* best-seller, the next day on the sale pile at the bookstore. Good literature, like the works of Shakespeare, Chaucer, John Updike, Robert Frost, Annie Dillard, Truman Capote, Gabriel Garcia Marquez, Pablo Neruda, have lasted a long time. Good literature might delight, but it also challenges us and calls into question our ideas about sexuality, race, gender, politics, religion, and faith. Good literature is provocative. It challenges and provokes, makes us think outside the box. Most people don't want to come home and read all 800 pages of *War and Peace*, *The Brothers Karamazov*, or *Les Misérables*. It's much easier to pick up a Harlequin romance or mystery novel, read it in two days and then begin another one. Some of the best literature, in fact, is contained right in the Bible. The Bible is the Word of God, but it is also literature, and some of the best literature too. That is why many colleges, even secular universities, offer courses on the Bible as literature.

If we want to be provoked and challenged, we just have to open up the Gospel of Matthew. In the first page, we read about intrigue, murder, suspense, mystery, and romance. It's got the best of both pulp fiction and literature. We read about the young Mary who has conceived of the Holy Spirit and will have a baby. Then Joseph wants to divorce his wife and leave her for the sake of social propriety. There are wise men who come and go out of the blue neither revealing who they are, where they are from, or where they are going. Then there is King Herod, one of the greatest kings of his time, right in the middle of this intrigue, jealous of the infant Jesus. So much ambiguity in this passage, so much we don't know, so many strands of story line left undone. If I had written this story, I would have had Joseph falling in love with Mary and having a baby the old fashioned way; the baby Jesus growing up in Nazareth, and they would have all lived happily ever after. But then again I am not the author of this story and we know that it doesn't turn out this way. But we want this story to work out because we are not comfortable living with ambiguity. We want closure. We want certainty. We want to know that things will turn out well.

Trust me, I'm not comfortable with ambiguity either. There were two particular times in my life when I had a really difficult time with faith. The first was when we decided to move to this parish. I had a choice of going to a large parish in eastern Pennsylvania with a four-bedroom brick rectory and a low salary or come to Charlotte with a small community, no rectory, and even less pay. I went back and forth, sleepless nights and all, clammy hands, and then finally a friend of ours said sometimes you just have to fall into the hands of God and trust. That's what faith is about. I asked her, "But are you sure things will turn out in Charlotte?" "No," she said, "I'm not sure." I said, "What do you mean that you're not sure?" I'm not sure what she said but it was probably, "Bill, what part of that don't you understand?" But I did fall into God's hands, and while the story isn't over yet, I think I made the right choice, at least the right choice from my perspective.

The other time of great ambiguity was sitting with my dying mother in a nursing home. Anyone who has had to stay with a suffering friend or relative knows the agony and stress of watching someone die slowly. She was suffering from liver disease. There I was, questioning God and my faith. People told me that things would turn out okay, but okay for whom? They said those things and walked away, but I had to remain and take care of my mother. To sit with someone in their pain and suffering and not walk away, that's faith. That's trust, and I think that is what we are called to do as disciples, to trust God even when we haven't got the foggiest idea of what our life will be like. We just put one foot in front of the other, trusting that Jesus knows more than we do.

If I was the author of my mother's story, she wouldn't have died from liver disease, in a nursing home, at fifty-eight years of age. She would be here today watching her grandchildren grow up, buying presents at Christmas, attending graduations and weddings, and strolling off into the sunset. But I'm not the author of her story, just like I'm not the author of the gospel reading. Our stories are not finished. They are a work in progress and as a work in progress we just have to keep at it putting one foot in front of the other until that final day.

FOOD FOR THOUGHT

1. Many people want easy answers to their questions. They want a God who will dole out quick "fix its" to our problem. The spiritual life is not like that. More often than not we have to live with ambiguity and mystery. Life is not always neat and easy. It's messy. What are the messy parts of your life? How do you deal with ambiguity?

2. Matthew says that the three wise men from the East came bearing gifts for the Christ child. God has given us so many gifts and talents. Which gifts will you offer Jesus this year? How can you better serve Him in both word and deed?

3. Read: Isaiah 55:8–9, Luke 2:19, Matthew 11:3.

CHAPTER NINE

DON'T BOTHER ME, I'M BUSY

One of the dinner guests, on hearing this, said to Him, "Blessed is anyone who will eat bread in the Kingdom of God!" Then Jesus said to him, "Someone gave a great dinner and invited many. At the time for the dinner, he sent his slave to say to those who had been invited, 'Come; for everything is ready now.' But they all alike began to make excuses. The first said to him, 'I have bought a piece of land, and I must go out and see it; please accept my regrets.'" (Luke 14:15–18)

I went to school in south central Pennsylvania, which many people called "God's Country." They called it God's Country because of the vast farmlands and beautiful open spaces. Our college apartment bordered the back of the college, which was adjacent to a series of rolling hills. Farmers grew wheat, soybeans, and tobacco. After class, my friend and I would get on our bikes and ride down the curvy roads just to see those farms, especially the old red barns and white farm houses with wooden porches and swings in the front yard. During the late autumn months, the farmers harvested their crops and we'd see freshly picked tobacco hanging upside down in the barns, drying.

This was God's country, but it was also Amish country. I lived just outside of Lancaster, Pennsylvania. Every day we would see a horse and buggy going down the road, or we would certainly see one tied up in the traditional horse stall in front of the supermarket. The amazing thing about the Amish is their strong sense of community. If a newly married couple needed a new barn, there would be a barn raising. Everyone from the surrounding area would come and help. It was not uncommon to have one or two hundred people — men, women, and children arriving ready to work and of course ready to eat. They would have chicken, roast beef, vegetables, and plenty of ice tea and pie. There was no need for mortgages, for hiring a contractor, or for obtaining building permits. Everyone would just come and help. Some would bring the wood, others would bring tools, and others would bring food. The wives would take care of the children. A barn could go up in a day or perhaps two depending on how much work they could accomplish.

I had a family friend who lived in Kuwait. The husband had a very good job as an engineer. They had two little children who attended good schools. They were very safe and secure until one day Saddam

Hussein decided to invade Kuwait. The soldiers seized their bank accounts, took their money, their houses, their lands, and their properties. My friend and his family had a choice: they either could stay in Kuwait and live in utter poverty or they could move to the United States.

They had a cousin in South Carolina who invited them to live with her. She had no husband or children, so she had plenty of space for her cousins. Now most people I know would probably help these folks too, perhaps a week or two at the house, a few home cooked meals, do their laundry, and give them some money to get back on their feet. But most folks would not do what this lady did. These people stayed not just for a week, not just for a month, but for an entire year. Why so long? Well, they had to get established. The husband needed a job, the children needed to enroll in school; they had to save money for their own house. When I asked her why she didn't ask her family to leave sooner, she said, "How could I? I'd be ashamed to send them away. I had to help."

Isn't that what a parish community is all about, helping each other? After all, members of a parish come together every Sunday and say the same prayers, recite the same hymns, receive the same bread and wine from the same chalice. After services, we share fellowship with one another. Isn't our life about our common fellowship or "communion" with one another? This call for mutual support is ongoing, like in the gospel lesson from Luke. This wealthy man was frustrated because the people whom he invited didn't want to come to his party. They had better things to do; one had a new wife, another had bought some land, and another needed to check on his cattle. They all had excuses. When the man heard these excuses, he commanded his servants to keep going further, keep inviting people to come to his banquet. He told them to go to the highways and the hedges and beyond. He didn't sit there and wallow in self-pity saying, "Woe is me. Woe is me." No, he kept calling more people so they could respond. St. Paul puts it another way in his Epistle to the Ephesians:

> *I, therefore, the prisoner in the Lord, beg you to lead a life worthy of the calling to which you have been called, with all humility and gentleness, with patience, bearing with one another in love, making every effort to maintain the unity of the Spirit in the bond of peace. There is one body and one Spirit, just as you were called to the one hope of your calling, one Lord, one faith, one baptism, one God and Father of all, who is above all and through all and in all.* (Ephesians 4:1–6)

We are all called, but sometimes we fail to respond. Life gets in the way. Yet the Lord doesn't give up on us, He keeps calling us to walk the walk of faith, to struggle and strive to follow Jesus, and along the way to support one another. We cannot live alone, we live life with other people broken and fallen as they are, as we are.

FOOD FOR THOUGHT

1. The wealthy man invited guests to his party. They all declined because they had excuses. Jesus calls us, just like the guests in the gospel reading. So often, just like the guests, we have excuses too. Take some time and think about your life. What are the excuses that you use not to follow Jesus in your daily walk of faith?

2. The wealthy man in the gospel reading also showed great hospitality. He put on a large party for strangers. Every Sunday Jesus puts on a beautiful banquet for us which we call the Lord's Supper. He is the great High Priest who sets the table, who invites us, who provides the food and the drink. Take some time and say a prayer of thanksgiving to God for His always feeding and providing for us as we are spiritually nourished to keep moving forward.

3. Read: Psalms 145–148, John 17, Luke 24.

CHAPTER TEN

FINAL EXAM

When the Son of Man comes in His glory, and all the angels with Him, then He will sit on the throne of His glory. All the nations will be gathered before Him, and He will separate people one from another as a shepherd separates the sheep from the goats, and He will put the sheep at His right hand and the goats at the left. Then the king will say to those at His right hand, "Come, you that are blessed by My Father, inherit the kingdom prepared for you from the foundation of the world; for I was hungry and you gave Me food, I was thirsty and you gave Me something to drink, I was a stranger and you welcomed Me." (Matthew 25:15–30)

Springtime means green grass, blooming flowers, migrating birds, and graduation time. But before you get to graduation, you have to go through final exams. Most students do not like final exams very much, staying up late studying and cramming for tests, reading extra books, and reviewing notes. At my seminary graduation, I remember the dean saying, "Well, I have good news, and I have bad news," and, of course, we all wanted to hear the good news first. So he said, "Okay, the good news is that you passed all your classes: Scripture, Liturgy, Theology, and Church History. You finished your volunteer work, you completed all your chapel requirements, and most importantly, you passed your exams. You'll be good priests one day. The bad news is that you are now responsible for all of this information!" And we turned to one another like what is he talking about. You are responsible for all the information that you learned and you are accountable for it. And this was really made clear to me at my ordination. During the ordination service, the bishop puts a little piece of holy bread in your hands and says, "Receive this pledge and preserve it whole and unharmed until the second coming of Christ." The priest is responsible for all of this, and by extension we are too. We are responsible for each other and for the entire Church.

The long reading from Matthew is like our final exam. Our judgment will be based on one thing and that one thing is love. In this passage, we read about the naked, those in prison, the sick, the suffering, the hungry, and the thirsty. Matthew doesn't mince words. He wants us to know what is really important in life. He is so adamant about this that he repeats these themes four times in the reading. Our judgment will be on how well we show love. It's easy to say I love you, to send a card or give a box of chocolates, but it's much harder to sit with someone who is sick and suffering and just be with them knowing that there is nothing you can do to make them feel better. There is nothing you can do to save them, you just have to sit there and show compassion. That is the basic form of love. Loving someone but not receiving love in return seems nearly impossible, and it is.

There was a story that one of my priest friends told me a long time ago. He was a priest in New York City, in a very large parish. People were coming and going all the time. One evening after Vespers, he noticed an older lady sitting in the back. She did not look familiar. After Vespers, he had adult education class, a Bible study, or an open discussion. On this particular evening, after his Bible study, this lady stood up and said in her thick New York accent, "Father, do these parishioners really believe what you're teaching because I've lived on this block for a long time now and I really don't see any works of mercy being done here." After she was done, she got up and walked out the door. My friend felt like he got kicked in the stomach, such a powerful statement from an old lady. It turned out that this lady was Dorothy Day, the famous social organizer and lover of the poor who started the *Catholic Daily Worker* and houses of hospitality in New York City and is now up for canonization in the Roman Catholic Church. She didn't take any money from the Church but collected donations from all types of people. She ministered to drunks, druggies, prostitutes, widows, and street people. She served soup, bread, and coffee. She had a priest come and celebrate the services. She had only one rule in her shelter: you cannot hurt anyone.

One of my favorite quotes about prayer is from Frederick Buechner, "follow your prayer." If we pray in the Lord's Prayer, "on earth as it is in heaven," then our life should follow that, shouldn't it?

FOOD FOR THOUGHT

1. This reading from Matthew is very long. Take some time and re-read it. Make a note of anything particular that you notice.

2. Make a list of all the various ways that you help other people. Is there anything else that you can be doing but are not currently doing? Make a list of your parish ministries too. Maybe your parish community can increase the number of outreach ministries to the local community.

3. Read: Mark 13, Luke 19:1–10, 1 Corinthians 3:10–12.

CHAPTER ELEVEN

JESUS IS MY FRIEND

This is My commandment, that you love one another as I have loved you. No one has greater love than this, to lay down one's life for one's friends. You are My friends if you do what I command you. I do not call you servants any longer, because the servant does not know what the master is doing; but I have called you friends, because I have made known to you everything that I have heard from my Father. You did not choose Me, but I chose you. And I appointed you to go and bear fruit, fruit that will last, so that the Father will give you whatever you ask Him in My name. I am giving you these commands so that you may love one another. (John 15:12–17)

September is back-to-school time, and I always love this time of year. My mom would go shopping for new jeans and sneakers and usually a new backpack and school supplies. I enjoyed summer vacation, but I always liked September. It was good to see my old friends again and to make new ones.

Making friends, though, is a tricky business. Things usually go well in the beginning, but then you have your first argument or maybe you get jealous. After all, we are human and these are typical human reactions. I had a good friend named Jerry, and Jerry and I did everything together. I mean everything! We played soccer, we rode our bicycles around town, and we walked and hiked along trails. We were inseparable. We always got along, and we never had a fight. Well, not until Alex came to town. Alex was the new kid on the block, new to the neighborhood and new to our school. Jerry and Alex quickly became friends, and I was very jealous. Alex had a new stereo system. He had a computer. He was cool. Jerry invited me to play with Alex, but I always said that I was busy. Actually, I wanted to play, but I wanted Jerry all to myself. After a while, I decided to give it a try and be friends with Alex. I realized that he was a nice kid and the three of us got along just great.

When I was younger, I thought Jesus was great. He cured the sick. He walked on water. He raised the dead. Jesus was my super-hero. But then He goes ahead and says something like He does in the gospel, like love your enemies and always be generous. Does Jesus really expect me to love my enemies, do good, and always be generous? This goes against our human nature. When you're in the lunch line and someone cuts in front of you, your first reaction is not to say, "Okay, why don't you go ahead of me." Usually the answer is, "Beat it buster, go to the end of the line and wait like everyone else." Or, "it's not fair, I've been waiting longer than you have." When someone hits you on the playground, the first reaction, our human nature reacting, is to hit the other kid back. The way of the world is an eye for an eye and a tooth for a tooth. You get me, I'll get you even better. How many times have you been in an argument and at the end of it you say, "I told you so" or "I knew that I was right." It feels good to relish someone else's pain.

Yet Jesus raises the bar for discipleship. If we want to be His friend, we had better be able to change our ways. Jesus bothers me. Before, he was my friend, but I'm not sure anymore. It's too hard. Who wants to be nice all the time? To love people, about whom we really don't care? Paul says the same thing in his epistle to the Corinthians, "My grace is sufficient for you, my power is made perfect in weakness." Weakness, are you kidding? No, Paul is dead serious. Weakness.

Paul was complaining about some ailment. We have no idea what it was. Some say that Paul was short of stature and that he had this Napoleon complex about him, that he was embarrassed because of his height. Others say that Paul had a speech impediment. However, we really don't know the specifics of his problems. Yet whatever this ailment was, he asked the Lord to remove it and three times the Lord said,

"My grace is sufficient for you, my power is made perfect in weakness." I guess God was making a point here, no matter how hard or long Paul prayed he would still struggle with that nasty thorn.

We have all had moments when we were down and out; times when we couldn't take it any longer. I just met a friend of mine who is a construction worker. He was telling me about his current job, but then before we parted, he asked me to pray for him. When I inquired about the reason, he said that he was being laid off for the second time this year. He has a wife and three children and a baby due in two months. I can't imagine what is going through my friend's head. He has a mortgage payment, a car payment, food, utility bills, and student loans. He said that unemployment only pays a portion of your salary, not all of it. Maybe you have been in a similar predicament. Maybe you have been close to losing your job. Maybe you have had to watch a parent or a friend die. Maybe you had some tragic time in your life which got the best of you. As Paul reminds us, "My grace is sufficient for you, my power is made perfect in weakness."

There have been many times in my life when I felt so weak that I could not go on anymore. There were a few times in parish ministry when things got so bad I thought, "Why am I doing this? Why am I staying in the parish?" I was tired of all the complaining. Tired of the stress. Tired of the lack of volunteers. All I wanted was to pack my bags and get out of town. Well obviously I didn't leave, because I'm still here. It was one of those times when Paul's words rang true, "My grace is sufficient for you, my power is made perfect in weakness." It was one of those times when I wished Jesus wasn't my friend. It was so hard being weak, feeling so little and so very lost. Yet God was with me. He was closer than I could have ever imagined. I thought I was all alone in my deep and dark night, yet God was still with me. Like a good friend, He never left my side, and you can believe that I am so glad He stayed.

FOOD FOR THOUGHT

1. Jesus expects a lot from us. He raises the bar for discipleship. Too often we want to lower the bar. Hopefully, we will strive to follow Jesus the best that we can each and every day, through good times and bad, through joy as well as sorrow.

2. The world upholds strength, not weakness, as an important character trait. Yet our God is the opposite. Saint Paul tells us that our real power is made perfect through our weakness. This is often difficult for us to accept. But God's ways are not the ways of the world!

3. Read: 1 Corinthians 13, 1 John 4:7, Colossians 3:14.

CHAPTER TWELVE

AND SOME DOUBTED

Now the eleven disciples went to Galilee, to the mountain to which Jesus had directed them. When they saw Him, they worshiped Him; but some doubted. And Jesus came and said to them, "All authority in heaven and on earth has been given to Me. Go, therefore, and make disciples of all nations, baptizing them in the name of the Father and of the Son and of the Holy Spirit, and teaching them to obey everything that I have commanded you. And remember, I am with you always, to the end of the age." (Matthew 28:16–20)

Many young moms and dads often have just a smidgen of doubt as they await their newborn child. I remember those days well. My wife was several months pregnant and we were young and excited and scared. I was going to be a new daddy and thought, "I can't be a dad. I don't know how to change diapers, when to burp and when not to burp, or how or when to feed the baby." Babies don't come with instruction manuals. But there I was just a few weeks shy of having my life changed forever.

Many people have doubts about what next week, next month, or even next year will bring. Perhaps your company told the employees that they will be downsizing next year. Every week you wait for a pink slip. How many people wonder whether or not they will have a job next year? How many senior citizens worry about having enough money in their 401K? What about those whose retirement is only months, or a few years off. Will they get to retire, or will they have to keep on working? There is a lot of fear, anxiety, and doubt in our world.

Most of us deal with all kinds of doubt in our life, whether about our parenting skills, job security, or even about God. How many of us have doubted God's work in the world? What about that nice neighbor down the street, the one who always smiles when you see her and is so kind as to watch your dogs when you go out of town, or the neighbor who keeps her lawn looking nice? One day you hear that she has come down with a rare form of cancer, it's ripping through her body. You shake your fists at God and yell and shout at Him, "How can this be Lord, how can this be?" Every day cold-blooded killers get off on legal technicalities, drug dealers roam the streets, and Wall Street executives keep getting windfall bonuses, yet this wonderful lady gets the short shrift. She gets cancer and everyone else is flying high. You question God. You ask yourself, why should I believe at all? We have all walked down this road, some longer than others. If we take our life seriously, then questions will certainly arise.

But we are not alone. Matthew ends with a one-line zinger. Every time I read this passage, I stop for a minute and re-read it, "They worshipped Him, but some doubted." Doubted? Did Matthew write that? Maybe he was supposed to say, "believed" or "had faith." I looked through several Biblical commentaries and they all say that the disciples doubted. It's there in black and white.

How could the disciples doubt? After spending three years following Jesus around Galilee and Judea, after witnessing miracles, after hearing Him preach the gospel. Jesus couldn't have done anything differently. He changed water into wine, He multiplied the loaves and fishes, and He even raised the dead. Even after all of this, Matthew says that the disciples doubted.

I guess it is possible to doubt Jesus. There is no certainty in life, is there? Thomas had trouble believing. So did John the Baptist, which is even more striking since John and Jesus were cousins. John was holed up in prison and at one of his low moments in life he told his disciples to go to Jesus and ask if He were the messiah or if they should look for another. This is John the Baptist, not just anyone, but the one who was born while his mother was still barren and advanced in years, the one who baptized Jesus, the one who proclaimed the Kingdom of God with power, the one who ate locusts and wild honey while walking around in sheep skins. If John had trouble believing, I guess we're in good company.

Last year I was reading Mother Teresa's journals. Teresa was a firebrand. She left her comfortable life in a cloistered monastery in northern India for a life-long ministry serving the poor in the Calcutta slums. She devoted her life to helping children who made a living through prostitution and dumpster diving. She helped raise young children and cared for the sick and dying. While reading her daily diary entries, I was very surprised by the numerous entries about doubting the Lord. Mother Teresa had long periods of great doubt and darkness, what the Spanish mystic St. John of the Cross called, "The dark night of the soul." St. John of the Cross had long periods in his life where he felt God abandoned him, echoing the words of Psalm 22, "My God, my God why hast Thou forsaken me?" (Psalm 22:1). Like John of the Cross, Teresa felt spiritually tortured. She had long periods where she felt alone, alone without the soothing presence of God's hand on her. So often Teresa said that she just wanted to give it all up. Yet she continued in her walk of faith, even though it was filled mostly with darkness and doubt.

Faith is about putting one foot in front of the other despite not seeing the end of the road. Faith is about following God's still small voice that calls and invites us to keep walking. We put our trust in something without being able to touch, taste, or feel it. It's crazy really, yet for two thousand years that is what Christians have been doing. I guess we are not alone then in this walk of faith. We keep going, hand in hand with those who have gone before us, and those who will come long after us.

Food for Thought

1. Have you had times of doubt and despair? Have there been rough patches in your life where you struggled with your faith? Take some time and write these experiences down. See if you see any patterns emerging.

2. Faith is hard for all of us. The Scriptures remind us that we are not alone. Abraham, Moses, David, John the Baptist, Thomas, and even St. Paul had trouble along the way. We all struggle from time to time. When you feel down and out, when you feel like you're alone, remember that as a Christian you are part of a large community of believers who, just like you, struggle with their faith.

3. Read: Psalm 22, Matthew 28:16–20, John 14:14–17.

CHAPTER THIRTEEN

EVERYTHING IS FROM GOD

Once while Jesus was standing beside the lake of Gennesaret, and the crowd was pressing in on Him to hear the word of God, He saw two boats there at the shore of the lake; the fishermen had gone out of them and were washing their nets. He got into one of the boats, the one belonging to Simon, and asked him to put out a little way from the shore. Then He sat down and taught the crowds from the boat. When He had finished speaking, He said to Simon, "Put out into the deep water and let down your nets for a catch." Simon answered, "Master, we have worked all night long but have caught nothing. Yet if you say so, I will let down the nets." (Luke 5:1-5)

There are a few things in life that I find very boring. Baseball is one of them. A few years ago, some parishioners wanted me to go with them to a minor league baseball game. I really didn't like baseball, but because I was their pastor I accompanied them. I bought a hotdog and a soda, and about three innings into the game, I leaned over and asked a parishioner, "Is the game almost over?" He looked at me with a smile and said, "Well, Father, there are seven innings left. Just be hopeful they don't go into extra innings." I shrugged my shoulders and ate the last bite of my hot dog. For the life of me, I didn't understand why these grown men took so long to hit a ball and run around in circles. My one-year-old daughter did that at home and I didn't have to pay to watch her.

I also find fishing boring. My wife loves fishing. When we were first married, I went fishing with her. All you do is sit in the hot sun, with a worm on the end of your fishing line and you wait and wait and wait until a fish decides whether or not to eat that worm.

One year during our annual beach vacation, we went to the local fish camp to have lunch. It's located on a small harbor where you can watch boats coming in and out. As we were eating, I noticed a small charter boat coming in to dock. The boat docked and only one man got off. He had a large grin on his face, and he was holding a small plastic grocery bag. He strolled over to the front of the dock where the captain had put a wooden plank to fillet the fish. The man put his hand into the bag and pulled out just one fish. The captain filleted the fish, gave it back to the man, and the man walked away towards the parking lot. I sat there is disbelief. This man was out in the ocean for probably two hours or more and only caught one fish. I thought to myself that this fish must have been the most expensive fish ever caught.

At the beginning of Jesus' ministry, we see Him at the shore with Peter, James, and John. They were fisherman, and they weren't fishing for pleasure. They had to bring in fish to feed their families, to support their coworkers, to pay for the upkeep of the boats and to buy more fishing equipment, fishing was their livelihood. At one point, Jesus told Peter that he should let down his net. Peter didn't respond, "Oh sure Jesus, we'll just put down our nets over here." No way, he said like a five-year-old, "We fished all night and caught nothing. Why do you want us to let down our nets again? That's a big fat waste of time." Yet Jesus told Peter, "Let down your nets for a catch." So Peter did as he was told. He was probably tired and hungry for a full Galilee breakfast of tea, cheese, bread, and olives and surely he missed his family. But Peter, James, and John let down their nets for a catch and Luke says that not only did they catch fish but they caught so many fish that the boats began to sink. Peter can't win. Either there are not enough fish or there are too many. After Peter and his crew have caught all those fish, Jesus tells them that no longer would they be catching fish but they'd be catching men. Jesus is not interested in regular fishing. He is interested in fishing for souls, catching people for the Kingdom.

We are reminded that it is God who is the source

of all things. Before, Peter and James and John could do nothing on their own. Only when Jesus arrived on the scene did they begin catching fish, a theme woven throughout the entire New Testament. Every time the disciples preached the gospel, the Bible tells us that hundreds believed and were saved. They came to join the new Christian community. But the disciples did not grow the Church. They preached the Gospel, and God grew the Church. Paul puts it another way. In his letter to the Corinthians, he tells them that he planted, Apollos, Paul's coworker, watered, but God gave the growth. It is God's Church, and He grows it, not us. We have to be careful about that, as soon as we think we are the source of all things we are doomed. We begin to fail.

God has a very funny sense of humor. Believe me, being a pastor reminds me of that all the time. Before being assigned to my current parish, I was invited to come and serve and preach a sermon. I was planning on leaving on a Friday. The day before, on Thursday, I came down with a nasty head cold, the kind where your nose runs, eyes water, and you sneeze a lot. Then on Friday, I lost my voice. On Friday night, I started coughing. On Saturday evening, we had a potluck supper and a meeting. The parish council was there. After I managed to make a short presentation, I opened it up for questions. A man in the back of the room raised his hand and asked, "We just heard everything you said. I just have one question: can you grow our parish?" I looked around at all these people. I thought that if I answered no, they probably wouldn't hire me. They would think, "this guy is lazy," and would look for someone else. If I said yes and in a year or two the Church hadn't grown, I'd be out of a job. So I gave a pastorally correct answer: maybe. When I said that, the man said, "Maybe? What kind of answer is that? I asked you a yes or no question." I responded by telling him that I would be the best pastor that I could be. I would preach the gospel, teach the faith, and serve the Lord. Of course, the parishioners help me in this effort but it was up to God if this parish would grow or not. It's been over ten years now and I'm still at the parish, so something is going right. We cannot give the growth, only God does. We can love, serve, forgive, and show mercy towards others and leave the rest to God.

Again, we look to Paul as an example. Paul didn't grow each of those Christian communities. He went around proclaiming the good news of Jesus Christ, telling people about Jesus and His work and His death and resurrection, and of course, he had help doing that, but in the end it was up to God to grow those Churches. Paul even says at one point—a verse that I always keep in my mind—"It is not I who live, but Christ who lives in me." Yes, it is not I who grow the Church. It is God who grows His Church. The more I decrease my ego and self centered will, the more God will grow and live in me and the more God-like I will become. The less there is of my fallen part, the more God's saving hand will help.

FOOD FOR THOUGHT

1. Fishing requires a lot of patience and a lot of faith, especially if you are fishing on a big lake. Take some time and think about your life and how hard it is to trust in the Lord. What is preventing you from following Jesus right now?

2. Being a Christian requires a lot of work on our part. It's hard to keep loving, serving, forgiving, and sharing and often getting nothing in return. Yet we must continue moving forward. We must struggle ahead. God will give the increase, we just have to trust in Him.

3. Read: James 1:1–9, Galatians 5:22–23, 1 Corinthians 13:1–13.

CHAPTER FOURTEEN

MOVING MOUNTAINS

*Jesus answered, "You faithless and perverse gen-
eration, how much longer must I be with you?
How much longer must I put up with you? Bring
him here to me." And Jesus rebuked the demon,
and it came out of him, and the boy was cured
instantly. Then the disciples came to Jesus pri-
vately and said, "Why could we not cast it out?"
He said to them, "Because of your little faith. For
truly I tell you, if you have faith the size of a mustard seed, you will say to this mountain, 'Move
from here to there,' and it will move; and nothing
will be impossible for you."* (Matthew 17:17-21)

When I was in seminary, we had classes and
chapel services from Monday through Friday,
but the weekends were free. Some students would go
over to the local Roman Catholic seminary and go
swimming. Others would go to the local mall and
take in a movie or go shopping. Some would take a

drive to the north shore of Long Island and go wine tasting. Others, like myself, would go to the local state park and go hiking.

One day, four of us went hiking. We all planned to go to the Divine Liturgy in the morning and then afterwards change into hiking clothes and take a leisurely hike. After the hike, we planned to come home and make dinner. Or so I thought.

We drove to the state park, parked the car and began our hike. It was an easy, nicely paved hiking path, just the kind for a guy like me, from New Jersey. At one point, one of my friends looked up and said, "Hey, let's hike up the mountain." I looked up to what was a very big mountain. No way, I thought. I had forgotten that when she was younger, she lived in Colorado, and in Colorado everyone goes hiking. So we started out. It was easy at first. There were plenty of rocks and small trees to hang on to. Then it got harder, the incline increased. I started breathing heavily. At one point, I looked up and noticed how much further we had to hike. There was no way I could do it. It was also too hard to hike back down. I had no choice, I had to keep going. Near the top of the mountain, through a small grove of trees we saw a bunch of people looking down at us and pointing. I thought they were looking at something below us so I looked behind me too. No animals. No other hikers either. Then I realized they were pointing at us! When we got within earshot they hollered down, "How far did you guys hike down?"

We shouted back, "We didn't. We hiked up!" They couldn't believe it. When we got to the top we looked down and couldn't believe that we'd hiked all the way up the mountain. A simple leisurely one-hour hike turned into a three-hour adventure.

In this particular gospel reading, Jesus talks about moving mountains. He tells His disciples, "If you have faith as small as a grain of mustard seed, you can say to this mountain move and it will move." A mustard plant produces some really small seeds. If you buy Gulden's Mustard or French Dijon mustard, you will notice the mustard seeds. They sometimes get caught in your teeth. But Jesus says that if you have faith as small as a mustard seed, you can tell this mountain to move from here to there and it will. Now that's a powerful statement.

We all have mountains in our life. Some might be small rolling hills and others may be as tall as Mount Everest. These mountains get in our way of following Jesus. Sometimes our mountains are self-inflicted. As my mother used to say, a lot of the time we cause our own problems. Other times these mountains just appear out of nowhere. If we have faith, we can move them. Not too much faith is needed either, just a little bit.

If Jesus accuses His disciples of having little faith, what about us? Most of us lack faith. At least I know I do. Yet Jesus reminds us to keep putting one foot forward each day. We put Jesus in the center of our life and whatever gets in the way we have to remove it. We pray in the Lord's Prayer, "Thy will be done on earth as it is in heaven." Although most of the time we really mean my will. We want *our* plans, *our* agendas, *our* ideas to come to fruition, and more often than not they do not. "Thy will be done" means that we put Jesus first and foremost in the center of our life.

FOOD FOR THOUGHT

1. Jesus talks about even having faith as small as a tiny mustard seed is all that we need in life. Take some time to reflect on a mustard seed growing into a large tree. It only takes a little bit of faith, but if we cultivate that faith, it will certainly grow.

2. Take some time and identify the many mountains in your life right now. What are they? How can you move them out of the way?

3. Read: Luke 17:5–10, Ephesians 1:15, 2 Timothy 3:10.

CHAPTER FIFTEEN

KEEP A KNOCKIN'

Now there was a woman who had been suffering from hemorrhages for twelve years; and though she had spent all she had on physicians, no one could cure her. She came up behind Him and touched the fringe of His clothes, and immediately her hemorrhage stopped. Then Jesus asked, "Who touched me?" When all denied it, Peter said, "Master, the crowds surround You and press in on You." But Jesus said, "Someone touched me; for I noticed that power had gone out from me." When the woman saw that she could not remain hidden, she came trembling; and falling down before Him, she declared in the presence of all the people why she had touched Him, and how she had been immediately healed. He said to her, "Daughter, your faith has made you well; go in peace." (Luke 8:43–48)

Every once in a while I get irritated and angry. I usually don't get angry at family members, friends, or neighbors — but I do get angry at my lawn. Yes, you read it correctly, my lawn. Last spring we had our lawn aerated and reseeded. The landscaper pushed this loud machine across the lawn several times and then spread both grass seed and fertilizer. Before leaving, he told me that he sprayed some weed control in order to kill the weeds. I went to bed happy that I was going to have a green lawn.

I woke up the next day to a surprise. The grass wasn't green, not even a shade of green. My lawn was brown as coffee. I thought the man had spot sprayed my lawn, but he actually sprayed the whole thing. Everyone else in the neighborhood had green grass and I had a big brown lawn. Every day I woke up and looked outside for the smallest sign of life, but nothing happened. The lawn was still brown! Every day for ten days I woke up and looked outside and saw brown grass. Then I woke up and low and behold I saw tiny sprigs of green peaking out of the ground.

It takes a lot of patience waiting for grass to grow. We live in a culture that wants everything right away. With the internet, Facebook, and Twitter, we have information at the tips of our fingers, and we get it fast. If I need to know the author of a book, I can look it up on Google. It's hard waiting for things. It's hard waiting for grass to grow. It's hard waiting for lab results to come back after we've had blood work done.

It's hard waiting to hear back from an employer after we've applied for a job. Waiting is difficult, painful even, but wait we must.

I can only imagine how hard it was for this woman to wait for help. The gospel said that she waited twelve years to find healing and comfort from her blood hemorrhage. I can imagine her going from doctor to doctor seeking medical relief, always getting the same answer: "Sorry we can't help you. Try the doctor down the road." Again and again she heard the same answer, "no." Yet she didn't give up. She kept on searching and looking. Twelve years she had this flow of blood. She was so determined that she pushed and shoved people out of the way and touched Jesus' tunic and it worked. Her hemorrhaging stopped. Why did she think she was pushing and shoving those people to get to Jesus? She must have had a lot of patience.

Jesus reminds us that we need to be proactive, "Ask, and it will be given you; search, and you will find; knock, and the door will be opened for you. For everyone who asks receives, and everyone who searches finds, and for everyone who knocks, the door will be opened" (Matthew 7:7–8). My mom would translate that as "Take the bull by the horns." Very often Christians are too passive, sitting in our misery, feeling hopeless and helpless. We wait for an answer to fall from the sky into our lap. It doesn't happen like that. Jesus tells His disciples: "Ask and you will receive, seek and you shall find, knock and it shall be opened to you." Asking, seeking, and knocking is our prayer. These are active words, not passive ones. This old lady in the gospel was so tenacious she just wouldn't take no for an answer. Luke mentions an unnamed woman who bothered the local judge so much that he said I don't care if she is good or bad I will give her what she wants just so she will stop bothering me, "Though I have no fear of God and no respect for anyone, yet because this widow keeps bothering me, I will grant her justice, so that she may not wear me out by continually coming." That is what discipleship is, taking the walk of faith with boldness and courage, all the while asking, seeking, and knocking. Our answer may not come right away, like the woman in the gospel who had to wait twelve years to get her's. Sometimes the answer comes in a day, a month, or a year. Maybe a few years. Maybe decades. But it comes. Often the answer is right in front of us. Jesus is there all the time, but if we just stay put, nothing will happen.

One day I was reading some of Frederick Buechner's writing. Buechner is a pastor and a writer. I cannot remember where I read it or the exact quote but it goes something like this, "Follow your prayer." In other words, if you pray for peace, your job is to live and be peace to those around you. If you pray for unity, try to exhibit a spirit of unity and community to your family, friends, and coworkers. Live your prayers in your daily activities. What you pray with your lips, live with your body. That is really what asking, seeking, and knocking is all about, following your prayer to wherever it leads. You might surprise yourself in the process.

FOOD FOR THOUGHT

1. The walk of faith is more like a marathon than a sprint. We must have patience with ourselves as we go through life day by day.

2. The unnamed woman in Luke's gospel was stubborn. She was persistent in her badgering the judge. Are we persistent in our faith? Are we stubborn with God, always asking, seeking, and knocking?

3. Read: Matthew 6:30–33, 7:7–12; Luke 15:8–10.

CHAPTER SIXTEEN

TRANSFIGURATION

Six days later, Jesus took with Him Peter and James and John, and led them up a high mountain apart, by themselves. And He was transfigured before them, and His clothes became dazzling white, such as no one on earth could bleach them. And there appeared to them Elijah with Moses, who were talking with Jesus. Then Peter said to Jesus, "Rabbi, it is good for us to be here; let us make three dwellings, one for you, one for Moses, and one for Elijah." He did not know what to say, for they were terrified. Then a cloud overshadowed them, and from the cloud there came a voice, "This is My Son, the Beloved; listen to Him!" Suddenly when they looked around, they saw no one with them any more, but only Jesus. (Mark 9:1–8)

I have several friends who are teachers. They all tell me that kindergarten is the most difficult age group to teach. If you spend any time with four-and five-year-olds, you will see that they have ants in their pants! However, most children love story time.

I like stories too. One of my favorite stories is the *Hungry Little Caterpillar* by Eric Carle. When you go in the backyard in the summertime, you will see those short little brown or green caterpillars. All these caterpillars do all day is eat leaves and get really big and fat. One day a small little hungry caterpillar was so hungry that he ate one whole strawberry. On the next day, he ate two large kiwis. On the third day, he ate through three large cupcakes. On the fourth day, he ate through four huge chocolate bars, and on the fifth day, he ate through five bananas. Now the caterpillar was very, very tired, the same tired feeling that you get when you eat a big turkey dinner on Thanksgiving. All you want to do after dinner is sleep. So what did the caterpillar do? He spun himself a large cocoon so that he could sleep in peace. He slept for a long time. Then, after several days, out came a beautiful yellow and black butterfly that floated through the air so gently.

Butterflies are delicate and dainty. When you take one look at the caterpillar and one look at the butterfly, you may even wonder how these two creatures are related. Every single butterfly in your garden was once a little brown or green caterpillar, and every caterpillar that you see munching on those green leaves will one day become a butterfly; God certainly knows what He is doing!

Just before His last trip to Jerusalem, Jesus took Peter, James, and John and climbed up a mountain. Matthew doesn't tell us which mountain it was, but tradition states that it was Mount Tabor, a tall mountain not too far from Nazareth. As Jesus was speaking, all of a sudden, a cloud overshadowed the mountain and Jesus' face shone brighter than the sun. The voice from heaven said, "This is My beloved Son with whom I am well pleased, listen to Him." You might think, well so what? But this same voice is heard twice in the Gospel. Once at the beginning when Jesus was baptized, when we hear the same voice from heaven saying, "I have glorified it and will glorify it again," and then once again, now in the Transfiguration. We are reminded that we must listen to Jesus. I bet you didn't know, however, that the word that is used for a caterpillar becoming a butterfly is the same word that is used for Jesus' Transfiguration. It is the word *metamorphosis*. Metamorphosis means to change form or being. A caterpillar goes through a metamorphosis to become a butterfly.

Jesus stood on Mount Tabor glowing with brilliant light. We have the power to do the same. We can shine like Jesus if we want to. Jesus promises us this earlier in Matthew,

> *"You are the light of the world. A city built on a hill cannot be hid. No one after lighting a lamp puts it under the bushel basket, but on the lamp-*

*stand, and it gives light to all in the house. In the
same way, let your light shine before others, so
that they may see your good works and give glory
to your Father in heaven."* (Matthew 5:17)

Wow, we are supposed to shine like Jesus. Now that
is a huge undertaking. But do you know what? We all
have the potential to shine like Jesus and let people
see our light. Just as every caterpillar has the potential to become a delicate butterfly, so too does every
one of us have the potential to become like Christ.
A caterpillar doesn't need anything else to become a
butterfly. It is born with everything it needs, except,
of course, food and water. Everything a caterpillar
needs to become a butterfly is in it. At our baptism,
we are given everything that we need for our walk of
faith. God is so good to us. We need to let our light
shine bright, just like the sun and always give glory to
God for everything that He has given us.

FOOD FOR THOUGHT

1. Often, I feel like I'm in a rut. I feel like life is passing me by and nothing is happening. Yet God calls us to be transformed.

2. A caterpillar takes ten days to spin its cocoon and wait until it turns into a butterfly. Our walk of faith requires patience as we live each day. Patience is not easy but we need to have patience as we follow Christ.

3. Read: Isaiah 60:1, Matthew 5:16, John 8:12–30.

CHAPTER SEVENTEEN

KNOWING JESUS

As He approached Jericho, a blind man was sitting by the roadside begging. When he heard a crowd going by, he asked what was happening. They told Him, "Jesus of Nazareth is passing by." Then he shouted, "Jesus, Son of David, have mercy on me!" Those who were in front sternly ordered him to be quiet; but he shouted even more loudly, "Son of David, have mercy on me!" (Luke 18:35–40)

I find it amazing that you can spend time with someone and think that you really know them. I have met married couples who have been married forty and fifty years, and even after all that time, they still say that they learn something new about their husband or wife.

When you're dating someone, everything is nice. You go out to dinner, you go to the movies, you talk, you laugh, and then eventually you get married. No problem. Then you have a fight, not the usual argument about who takes out the garbage or cleans up after dinner, I'm talking about one of those World War III nuclear attacks with words flying and maybe a door or two slamming. And you stand there and look at your husband or your wife and you wonder, "Where did that come from?" I never saw that side of them before? The same with children. They are so cute and cuddly and warm and nice and then one day they'll grow up and say, "I don't like you," or maybe they'll slam the door in your face or maybe they'll stomp and want to run away.

Most people thought they knew who Jesus was, but in reading the gospels, we find out that they hardly knew Him at all. In the beginning of the gospels, Jesus starts His ministry, and one of the first things we hear about Him is, "is this the son of Joseph the Carpenter?" Later on in the gospels, Jesus walks on water and calms the storm, and His own disciples say, "Who is this that water and waves obey Him?" Even His friends don't know who He is. When John the Baptist was in prison, he wondered if Jesus was really the person who He said He was and he sends his disciples to see Jesus and they ask Him, "Are you the one to come or shall we look for another?" Jesus tells them, "Tell John that the dead are raised, the blind see, the deaf hear, and the dumb speak." Now if John doesn't know who Jesus is, something's wrong.

Yet you really can't blame the disciples because Jesus doesn't act normal, at least, not according to the "normal" of the first century. It was not common or even acceptable for a Jewish rabbi to be with a woman by herself, yet Jesus goes out of His way and speaks to the Samaritan woman at Jacobs' well. It was common for Jews to go the Temple in Jerusalem for pilgrimage, but it was not common for someone to take a chair and a whip of chords and drive out the moneychangers. It was not usual to break the Sabbath, the holy day of rest, yet Jesus broke the Sabbath all the time. Time and time again throughout the gospels, Jesus seems to go against every religious, social, and cultural norm, he breaks all the rules, he goes against the common expectations, no wonder His disciples scratched their heads wondering, "who is this guy?"

Yet Jesus comes so that we can know Him. Not just know things about Him, anyone can Google Jesus and learn that He was born in Palestine in the first century and that He was born of Mary and grew up in Nazareth and taught and then died. These are facts about Jesus that anyone can learn. I'm talking about *knowing* Jesus. Every time we gather for Sunday worship, we hear the gospel readings, and these readings are not just words about Jesus, rather, it is Jesus Himself who speaks to us, Jesus reveals Himself, makes Himself known to us in His life-giving Word. Every time we break bread and receive His body and blood, we are receiving not just bread and wine but Jesus Himself.

At the end of Luke's gospel, Luke and Cleopas

are walking from Jerusalem to Emmaus, a small village about seven miles from Jerusalem. They are saddened by the fact that their friend and master just died. They are sad, because they are grieving. As they were walking away, they were also talking and wondering what had happened to their best friend. Then out of the blue someone started walking with them, a stranger. This man wondered why these disciples were crying and upset. They told them about Jesus. It was getting late and they were hungry. They stopped and ate. After eating, this person, whom we later realize was the risen Lord, vanished just as He had appeared, and they said, "Our hearts burned within us" when He spoke to us. Later Luke says, "He was known to them in the breaking of the bread." What a beautiful passage, that the risen Lord was made known to them, that He revealed Himself to them in the breaking of the bread, in the eating and sharing of fellowship.

I hope that, as we struggle with daily challenges and choices that life presents to us, we come to know Jesus. Not just facts about Jesus, but, *know* Jesus. So that we, like Luke and Cleopas, might say that our hearts burn within us as well, as we break bread and come to a deeper knowledge of Jesus and His Father.

FOOD FOR THOUGHT

1. Even though we have eyes, we are blind to the people and events right in front of us. Take some time and practice seeing the world around you. When you take your dog for a walk or if you take your morning jog, pay attention to the birds, the grass, the trees, and the people that you see. There is a big beautiful world out there, a world that God made for us, yet we often don't see the beauty right in front of us.

2. Knowing Jesus is at the heart of our common life as Christians, we cannot let ourselves be distracted from this one essential thing.

3. Read: Matthew 4:19, 1 John 1:1–4, 1 Corinthians 2:1–2.

CHAPTER EIGHTEEN

LESS IS MORE

Jesus, looking at him, loved him and said, "You lack one thing; go, sell what you own, and give the money to the poor, and you will have treasure in heaven; then come, follow me." When he heard this, he was shocked and went away grieving, for he had many possessions. (Mark 10:21–22)

When a young couple is planning on buying a house, they can purchase a new house with new floors, carpets, fresh paint, new roof, and new plants in the yard where everything is new and nice and clean. Or they can find an old fixer upper, a house that's gone unsold, one that has character, but needs some tender loving care. The couple might think it's wonderful to buy an old house and fix it up. They might think that you can do it over several weekends, a little bit here and a little bit there. But it's not as easy as it may seem.

A few years ago, there was a movie called *The Money Pit,* starring Tom Hanks. He and his wife thought it would be great to buy a fixer upper and spend time together fixing it up. You think that you only need a coat of paint here or a new carpet, maybe a new fridge and some new flooring. But then you get into the house, and you begin to realize you're in over your head. You start removing the wood flooring and you see that there is black mold under the floor so you rip out the entire floor. Then you attack the walls with a little spackle here and some fresh paint there. Then you find out the wiring was installed in 1925 and you have to re-wire the entire house. You might find out that the plumbing is bad, so you have to rip out all the copper piping and install PVC pipes. There is one funny scene where Tom Hanks' wife is lying in an old-fashioned cast iron lion claw tub. All of a sudden the tub falls through the rotting wood floor and crashes two floors below. Tom Hanks can't sell the house because it's a money pit.

In some ways, Jesus tries to give the rich man in the gospel a brand new house with brand new carpet, appliances, paint, garage, and landscaping. He does it all for free too, debt free, no mortgage and no rent. However, the man prefers his own little dump, which he tries so hard to renovate, but gets nowhere. He thinks that he can do it all by himself but he cannot. The man confesses that he doesn't commit adultery, he doesn't murder, he doesn't cheat, he doesn't lie, and Jesus says, great man, you are doing really well, but you know what, you still need to sell your possessions and give to the poor and come follow Me. And what does the man do? He walks away sad because he cannot bear to change his life, or rather, have his life changed. He likes his life the way it is.

What a sad story. Ironically, similar stories are told and retold throughout the gospels. Many people heard Jesus' call to come and follow, but so many of them couldn't bear giving up their life. At one point in His ministry, Jesus is preaching in Galilee and people from all the towns and villages go out to meet Him. One person says, hey Jesus, I'll be there in a minute, I just have to bury my father and what does Jesus say, "Let the dead bury their own, come and follow." The man never followed.

In the sixth chapter of John's gospel, Jesus takes five loaves and two fish and multiplies them, a miracle of miracles. Jesus feeds five thousand people. The crowd cannot believe it; He's like a magician performing great miracles. But then Jesus starts to preach the Gospel, and the people don't like that one bit. They like the miracles, they like having their bellies full, but once Jesus starts preaching, watch out. He says that He is the bread from heaven and the living bread. He then says that whoever eats His flesh and drinks His blood abides in Him. One by one the people leave him until finally Peter is left hanging around all by himself and Jesus turns towards him and says, "Are you too going to leave me, Peter?" And Peter says, "Lord, where are we to go, You have the words of eternal life." Jesus has the words of eternal life. Yet all those other folks couldn't let go, they couldn't let go of their old ways of life, their old ways of thinking and doing things. They couldn't let go of their material possessions and their old traditions. Jesus called them to new life and they couldn't follow.

We have to let go of a lot of things. We have to let go of our pride and of our jealousy. A long time ago, I held a grudge against someone. Every time I saw this person, my heart burned within me. I was so angry. Yet after a while, I let it go and I felt free. We have to let go of our anger, of our pride, and of our fear.

Jesus calls us to let go of all those things that keep us from following. He wants us to let go of our anger, of our greed, of our envy, of our pride, of our ego, of our comfortable life. He wants us to leave all that behind so we can follow Him. He's offering the most beautiful house in the world, and we prefer our dump that we try with haste to renovate and fix up, but we wind up getting nowhere, maybe today we can take Jesus up on His offer.

FOOD FOR THOUGHT

1. Jesus encounters a rich man. Most of us are not millionaires, but I venture to say that we most likely have more income and material possessions than most people in the world. We have homes, cars, and plenty of our "creature comforts" to make us happy. Make a list of some of the things that you can do without. Maybe some time this week you can donate them to the local Goodwill or Salvation Army, lightening your load as we all follow Jesus.

2. Jesus' main message in all four gospels is "come and follow." It sounds so easy, but it's usually very hard. Make a list of the things right now in your life that are keeping you from being more faithful to Jesus and the gospel message.

3. Read: Luke 5:1–11, Matthew 10:1–10, John 1:43–50.

CHAPTER NINETEEN

LONELY

Then He led them out as far as Bethany, and, lifting up His hands, He blessed them. While He was blessing them, He withdrew from them and was carried up into heaven. And they worshipped Him, and returned to Jerusalem with great joy; and they were continually in the temple blessing God. (Luke 24:50-53)

There are several types of loneliness. The first kind is when you have a long day at work and you're responding to email messages, working on three projects at once, and returning phone calls. When you get home, all you want to do is sit down, put your feet up and have five minutes to yourself. You may even want a cup of coffee or tea. However, what usually happens is your kids come rushing to the door yelling, "Mommy, mommy, look at this" or "Daddy, daddy, you'll never guess what we did in school." They barrage you with names, dates, projects, and programs.

Your brain has a meltdown. You seek peace and quiet. No husband. No wife. No kids. No pets. Just you sitting alone in a comfy lounge chair.

Then there is the other kind of loneliness, the one where you feel a deep sense of absence or loss. There are three particular times in my life when I felt terribly alone. The first time was when I was five or six years old. My mother took me grocery shopping, and she sent me to get some milk. I went to get the milk, and when I returned, mom wasn't where I had left her. When you are five years old, three or four minutes feels like an eternity. I walked up aisle after aisle and then finally found her.

The second time I felt really alone was when my father died. I was eighteen years old. At first, parishioners and neighbors were very kind. They brought casseroles, sent us cards, and called at least once per week. After several weeks, the cards, calls, and casseroles slowed down. One week there were ten cards in the mail, then five, then three, and then none. After a while, the cards stopped altogether. I remember sitting home with mom on a Sunday afternoon. I was reading the paper and she was watching re-runs on television and it felt so quiet in the house. No more food, no more calls, no more cards. No one came by to visit. No one asked us how we were doing. We felt abandoned, lost, and very lonely.

The third time I felt alone was when mom dropped me off at college. Millersville University was only a three-hour car drive from our home in New Jersey, but it was far enough, especially when I didn't have a car of my own. Mom helped me move in. We unpacked a few boxes, set up my bed, and arranged the rest of the room. We went out to dinner at a local diner. After dinner, we said our goodbyes and then she drove home. The walk back from the parking lot to my dorm room was a long one. This was my first time living away from home. I didn't know anyone and they didn't know me. I felt like a stranger in a strange land. It was scary.

Luke doesn't give us many details, but surely the disciples felt very lonely after Jesus died. In the first chapter of Acts, we read that forty days after His resurrection, Jesus spent time with His disciples, eating with them, teaching them and encouraging their faith. Yet Jesus commanded them to go to the nearby village of Bethany. It was there on a mountain that Jesus ascended into heaven. The disciples must have felt pretty lonely, their best friend and teacher, the one who preached inspiring sermons, who cured and healed diseases, who taught about love, mercy, and forgiveness, was gone. He was not coming back, at least not soon.

However, Matthew gives us a slightly different version of the same story. He tells us that Jesus led His disciples to a high mountain and admonished them to go to all nations preaching and teaching the faith and baptizing. Jesus then said, "I am with you always to the close of the age." He left them with words of hope.

Surely we all have had times of bitter loneliness. There are times when we felt that no one cared or no one was around to help us. We have been lonely. Yet Jesus reminds us, that no matter the circumstances in which we find ourselves, He is always with us. Even though Jesus is no longer physically present with us, he is with us in His spirit, in the memory of the Church. He is with us in our common worship and in our prayer. He is with us in the Eucharist. His words abide with us in Scripture.

Even though my father is gone I often think of him. Sometimes it feels like he is in the same room with me now. I see his round face and his smile. I have no doubt that there will be many times when I feel utterly alone. But I also know, as both Luke and Matthew remind us, that Jesus is with us until the end of the world. That is enough to keep me going as I put one foot in front of the other, in our common walk of faith.

FOOD FOR THOUGHT

1. Take some time and reflect on your life. Take note of the key times when you were especially lonely. What were the circumstances? How did you get through the loneliness?

2. When I start feeling alone and sad, I remember that there are many other people just like me who are alone. Some are elderly who have no spouse or anyone to take care of them. Some are widows and widowers who are living alone. Others are single people who have no family. I usually offer a short prayer to God being thankful that He is always with me and that even though I might be alone I am connected to a much wider community in the world.

3. Read: Psalm 22, Mark 1:35, Luke 5:16.

CHAPTER TWENTY

LOSING JESUS

Now every year His parents went to Jerusalem for the festival of the Passover. And when He was twelve years old, they went up as usual for the festival. When the festival was ended and they started to return, the boy Jesus stayed behind in Jerusalem, but His parents did not know it. Assuming that He was in the group of travelers, they went a day's journey. Then they started to look for Him among their relatives and friends. When they did not find Him, they returned to Jerusalem to search for Him. (Luke 2:41-45)

A few years ago, our family went on a vacation to New Mexico. When we landed back in Charlotte, we decided that I would go get the car while my wife and two daughters stayed at the terminal. I hopped on the bus and found my way over to Long Term parking Lot 1.

The long-term parking lot is alphabetically divided into rows. I thought I remembered where I had parked the car, so I told the bus driver to let me off at a certain place and I walked up and down the aisle trying to find my car. No car. I walked up and down the next two rows and still I couldn't find my car. It was dark which also made it extra difficult. I panicked. I had the same type of panic when you lose your keys, or your wallet. My heart raced. I had sweaty palms. Strange ideas popped through my head as in, "Maybe someone stole my car?"

When reading the birth narratives, we learn that Joseph and Mary lost Jesus. Yes, you heard it correctly. Mary and Joseph lost Jesus! How could they lose Him? Luke tells us that after two days on the road from Jerusalem to Nazareth, Mary and Jesus realized they had forgoten Jesus. They quickly returned to Jerusalem and searched up and down the streets. They still couldn't find Jesus. Finally, they found Him. He wasn't on the playground. He wasn't at a cousin's house. He was in the Temple. Luke says that Jesus was preaching and teaching as the Jewish leaders sat and listened. Luke says that Jesus was going about His Father's business. Even at the tender age of twelve, Jesus knew what He was supposed to be doing.

This gospel has a parallel story later in Luke. Mary and her sister Martha are at home. Jesus is also there. Martha is in the kitchen fretting and anxious about what food she should serve, and I can imagine the commotion and noise in the kitchen as Mary sat quietly at Jesus' feet and listened to His teaching. Jesus tells Martha, "Mary has chosen the good portion that shall not be taken away from her." The good portion is sitting with Jesus and listening.

As disciples, we often forget that a basic part of the Christian life is sitting at Jesus' feet and listening. We often replace Jesus with other things. The biggest sin in the Bible is not sex, or adultery, or murder, or stealing, but replacing God with something or someone else. It's the First Commandment, "Thou shalt have no other Gods before Me." Jesus says the same thing in a slightly different way echoing the laws of the Old Testament, "You shall love your God with all your heart, with all your soul, with all your mind, and your neighbor as yourself." Powerful isn't it? Putting God back where He's supposed to be!

We often forget about God. I know I do. But God never ever forgets about us. We are always on His mind and that is why the Church always puts this reading before us, as a reminder not to lose God. We may lose Him, but He never loses us.

FOOD FOR THOUGHT

1. Mary and Joseph lost Jesus for a short time. It's hard to believe, but they did. Are there times when you felt you lost your faith? Are there times in life when you felt lost, off track? Take some time to explore why you got lost and how you found your faith in God again. You're not alone. There are many people who for one reason or another lost their faith or at least got sidetracked.

2. The Parable of the Prodigal Son is a story about losing and finding. Take some time to read this parable. With whom do you identify most?

3. Read: Luke 15:13–18, Matthew 18:12–14, John 10.

CHAPTER TWENTY ONE

SURPRISE, SURPRISE, SURPRISE

He entered Jericho and was passing through it. A man was there named Zacchaeus; he was a chief tax collector and was rich. He was trying to see who Jesus was, but on account of the crowd he could not, because he was short in stature. So he ran ahead and climbed a sycamore tree to see Him, because He was going to pass that way. When Jesus came to the place, He looked up and said to him, "Zacchaeus, hurry and come down; for I must stay at your house today." (Luke 19:1–5)

One day I was running some errands at the supermarket and while putting away the groceries I noticed the blinking red light on the answering machine. I thought it might be the local pharmacy calling about a prescription, or maybe it was a neighbor wanting to ask a question. I thought nothing of it until I pressed the play button. I couldn't believe it:

my college roommate from nineteen years ago had called and left a message. For some people, this might not be a big deal, but I hadn't heard from him in nineteen years: no email, no birthday or Christmas cards, nothing. He said that he was just thinking of me and wanted to see how I was doing. Talk about surprise and shock! It's the same feeling that you get maybe when a long lost friend or old coworker contacts you. It's a nice surprise, a little light for your day. The second thought that went through my mind though was "What does he want?" After all he must want something, that's why he's calling me!

This is the same surprise and shock that children have on Christmas morning when they walk downstairs in their bathrobes and see all the Christmas gifts under the tree: a new bike, a new dress, a doll, maybe a toy or a new game. Their eyes get so big and they jump up and down for joy. Or maybe it's the same surprise that children have when they ride a bike for the first time, or climb the monkey bars, or get an "A" on a spelling test or math test; the happiness and joy are so real, so powerful.

This is the same surprise and shock that Zacchaeus must have felt when Jesus came to Jericho and said to him, "Zacchaeus, today salvation has come to your house." Wow, salvation! I bet the crowds of people who heard Jesus probably scratched their heads and went "huh?" This guy is a crook, he works for the Romans, he cheats, he steals, he is a traitor, how dare Jesus go over to his house, this guy is nuts. Tax collectors were not model citizens either; they were Jews who worked for the Roman government. In return they were allowed to keep some of the tax money.

Yet Jesus still exclaimed that salvation had come his house. Jesus heard the magic words from Zacchaeus' lips, "If I defraud anyone, I return it fourfold and I give half of what I have to the poor." Most people couldn't say that; this Zacchaeus guy was on the right track. He was headed towards repentance.

Salvation has come to our house too. Every time we hear the gospel preached and proclaimed, salvation has come. Every Sunday we gather and hear the good news of the gospel, we are forgiven, we are saved. What great news, yet we'd rather believe in the daily news; the humdrum every day news: murders, rapes, wars, politics, lying, stealing, cheating, all the good stuff we read about online or in the daily paper. We've mixed up the daily news of this world with the good news of the kingdom. Jesus gives us the best news possible, new life in Him.

Food for Thought

1. Jesus surprised both the crowds and Zacchaeus. When we read the gospels, Jesus seems to surprise a lot of people. Does Jesus ever surprise you by His words or actions? When reading the gospels, does anything in particular strike you as interesting or intriguing? Take some time and make a list of the various things in the gospels that surprise you.

2. Zacchaeus told Jesus that He would restore people's money and make things right. Very often we hurt people, we do things that cause pain. Making amends is a very important part of the Christian life. This week try to make amends for the harm that you have caused others.

3. Read: Matthew 10:39, John 8:31, 15:1–11.

CHAPTER TWENTY TWO

CARRYING BURDENS

Truly I tell you, among those born of women no one has arisen greater than John the Baptist; yet the least in the kingdom of heaven is greater than he. From the days of John the Baptist until now the kingdom of heaven has suffered violence, and the violent take it by force. For all the prophets and the law prophesied until John came; and if you are willing to accept it, he is Elijah who is to come. Let anyone with ears listen! (Matthew 11:11–15)

One of my friends is a former soldier in the Marine Corps. The Marines are perhaps the toughest of all the armed forces. My friend said that the most challenging part about being a Marine was not the constant marching, camping, or drills, it was the mental things that caused the most grief. Every day they practiced shooting at the firing range until they improved their skills. They had to walk in formation and they couldn't turn their head when someone was talking to them. They were trained so well that when they went into battle, they didn't need to think about what to do, they just did it. The knowledge went from their head right to their heart. They lived, ate, and breathed the Corps.

The same thing happens with doctors. If you have a gall bladder attack, you will be rushed to the hospital and a doctor will perform surgery. The doctor will not look at that gall bladder and say, "Let me see, now what do I have to do?" No, they cannot afford to do that. Sometimes things go wrong in surgery and they have only a few minutes to fix the problem. Doctors are well trained so that an emergency, they immediately know what to do.

I had a cousin who studied music at Julliard. He said that when you attend a symphony or an opera, the music always sounds beautiful. The music sounds beautiful because every day the musicians practice their music. While taking a walk or riding on the subway, they go over the music in their head so that when the conductor starts with the first downbeat everything sounds majestic. Musicians train with both their head and their heart.

Jesus wants us to have heart knowledge. When Jesus began preaching, he didn't say, "Oh, first you ought to go to seminary and read a few books about my preaching." No, he simply said, "Come and follow." When He called His disciples, He didn't say,

"Gee, Peter, what do you think of Me?" or "Hey, John, do you like My miracles?" No, Jesus simply said, "Come and follow." And quite a few people heard that message but never followed. In one passage in the gospels, Jesus says, "Come and follow," and a guy responds, "But Jesus, I have to bury my father and then I'll come." Jesus says to him, "Let the dead bury their own." Then a rich man says to Him, "Jesus I'd love to come join You, but You know, I have this field over here and my animals and my investments." Jesus still says, "Come and follow." The message never changes. Jesus' simple message is to come and follow a message that is worth repeating.

Too often we carry so many burdens that weigh us down. These distractions often take us away from Jesus. The other day I saw someone driving a Toyota pick-up truck on the highway. He must have been moving because in the truck were a desk, a few lamps, a dresser. On top of all these things was a mattress that was tied with a rope. The truck was so heavy it was almost touching the ground. He certainly was carrying a heavy load. Jesus doesn't place heavy burdens on us, He simply invites us to come and follow. Jesus says that His yoke is easy and His burden light.

Yet our burdens weigh us down. We get angry. We get upset. We make up excuses. Or we follow part of the way and then drop off. Or we follow when it is convenient for us. Jesus' invitation is again announced, "Come and follow Me all of you who are heavy laden and heavy of heart and I will give you rest. My yoke is easy and My burden light." Come and follow. Will you accept His invitation?

FOOD FOR THOUGHT

1. Jesus calls out to us every day, "Come and follow." Do we?

2. Psalm 55:22 says, "Cast your burden on the Lord and He will sustain you." Many of us carry heavy burdens. Take some quiet time and make a note of your burdens. Ask God to help you carry them. Ask Him to help carry your heavy load as you walk the walk of faith.

3. Read: Psalm 51, Luke 17:20–37, Romans 15:10–17.

CHAPTER TWENTY THREE

MISSING THE OBVIOUS

There was a rich man who was dressed in purple and fine linen and who feasted sumptuously every day. And at his gate lay a poor man named Lazarus, covered with sores, who longed to satisfy his hunger with what fell from the rich man's table; even the dogs would come and lick his sores. (Luke 16:19–21)

After a long week at work, there's nothing better than watching your child play soccer with her friends. One particular Friday evening, I took my daughter to her game. The warm autumn sun was gently setting on the horizon and a crisp breeze was blowing. At one point during the game, I looked over and saw a guy staring at the ground. At first, I thought that he had dropped something. A few moments later I looked over and realized he was playing with his cell phone. Maybe he was checking his email, I thought. Then a few minutes later, I looked over and again his nose was in his phone. I couldn't believe it. This guy was spending his time on his cell phone and missing his daughter's soccer game.

So the game went on. Twenty minutes later, I looked over again and the guy was still playing with his cell phone. It was a high scoring game and all the children scored at least one goal. All of a sudden the ball came to his daughter and she kicked the ball hard and made a goal. Their team won the game. However, her dad had missed her goal. His face was planted in his phone.

It's easy to miss what's right under our noses. Once my wife told me to get her blouse from the laundry room. I walked upstairs, went into the laundry room, looked in the washing machine, in the dryer, through the hamper, and found nothing, "Honey, I don't see it," I yelled downstairs. She said, "It's up there, it's on the pile of clothes." I looked through the mountain of folded laundry. I saw socks, underwear, pants, but no blouse. "Honey," I yelled down to her, "I still can't find it." Then I heard the pitter-patter of her feet marching on those steps and with one huge swoop she picked up a pile of clothes and voila, her blouse was sitting there at the bottom of the pile of folded laundry.

We often miss the obvious. Jesus says as much in the Gospel. Luke tells us that every day the rich man walked past Lazarus who was lying right in front of his house. Ironically, Lazarus has a name while the rich man remains nameless. The rich man stands for any man. We are all the rich man; while we may not live in grandiose mansions with fancy cars, we are rich in so many ways.

The Gospel is not just about financial poverty either. There are many people who are living paycheck to paycheck and are one paycheck away from losing their home or car. There are single mothers who work two jobs just to feed their kids. There are families on WIC and who receive free butter and cheese. These are the Lazaruses of the world.

But Luke isn't just speaking about financial poverty, he speaks about spiritual poverty. Jesus talks about it in the Beatitudes, "Blessed are the poor in Spirit for theirs is the kingdom of heaven." Spiritual poverty means being empty. I've met many more people who are spiritually poor, people who lack love, compassion, and who walk around with no hope.

That's why hospitality is so important. In Judaism, the mother of the house always sets an extra place at the Sabbath meal for the Prophet Elijah. Elijah was an Old Testament prophet and represents the messiah. However, if you ask a rabbi why the wife sets out an extra place, he'll tell you it's in case a cousin or aunt comes by for Sabbath dinner. In the Christian tradition, we have a similar concept. In monasteries and in guesthouses, guests are supposed to be received and welcomed with love and treated like Christ.

Luke ends this gospel lesson with a powerful punch. All that fire and brimstone, enough to scare anyone! Our God is a God of love and truth and light, Jesus doesn't use this imagery to scare people into action. Rather He uses it as a forceful reminder that our faith is not just for our head, but it has to be lived in our hearts. Our faith has to work through our hands so that we love those who are poor. Hopefully this will open our eyes and our hearts to those who are poor in spirit and also open our hands to them, all of them, there are so many.

Food for Thought

1. We might not be materially rich, most of us don't live in large mansions and eat gourmet food every day but compared with the rest of the world we are very rich. Take some time and think about your life and make a list of all the riches you have.

2. The primary problem in this gospel story was that the rich man was oblivious to Lazarus' condition. It was his poor attitude towards him. Even in death the rich man thought he could order Lazarus around. May God help us see people in poverty, those who are spiritually poor as well as those in material need.

3. Read: Matthew 13:31–32, Matthew 25, Luke 19:1–10.

CHAPTER TWENTY FOUR

RAISING THE BAR

Then someone came to Him and said, "Teacher, what good deed must I do to have eternal life?" And He said to him, "Why do you ask Me about what is good? There is only one who is good. If you wish to enter into life, keep the commandments." He said to Him, "Which ones?" And Jesus said, "You shall not murder; you shall not commit adultery; you shall not steal; you shall not bear false witness; honor your father and mother; also, you shall love your neighbor as yourself." (Matthew 19:16–19)

September is back to school time. When I was in school, we received our report cards four times a year. It would come at the end of the day, and I couldn't wait to open it. I would walk home with a few of my friends and we'd open our report cards and compare them. When I arrived home, mom would already be there. She wanted to see my report card.

Once, when I gave it to her, I said, "So where is my $1.75?" Mom responded, "What do you mean $1.75?" "Well," I said, "Joey's mom gives him a dollar for an A, seventy-five cents for a B, and twenty five cents for a C, I should get a dollar seventy-five. "Not in this house. We don't get money for grades. If you want money, go live with Joey." My heart sank; all I could think about was getting a dollar seventy-five. Then she asked, "So why did you get a C in Science class?" I responded, "Well, science is hard and the teacher is boring and you know, it's just not an easy class." Then I tried justifying my grade, "But mom, a C is average, Joey got a C too." That didn't help. Then mom gave me the lecture that most parents probably give their children: "If you get average grades, then you'll go to an average college and then get an average job and earn an average salary and have an average life. Do you want an average life?" Oops, she hit a sore spot. Mom didn't settle for low expectations, she raised the bar. She could have easily let the C slide and who knows maybe in the future I would have gotten more Cs. Mom wanted me to do better; she wanted me to excel; she raised the bar.

Low expectations earn average results. The same goes for work. If your boss has low expectations, then the employees have low expectations too. During my college summer vacation, I worked for a landscaping crew. We worked from 9:00 AM until 5:00 PM. Around 4:40 PM, my supervisor started cleaning up and I said,

"John, we still have twenty minutes left to work" and he said, "No, we have to get back to the shop." So we packed up and got back to the shop. All the guys were waiting in line so that as soon as it was five o'clock they could punch out. The college didn't require overtime and they certainly were not going to give it.

Jesus raises the bar for His disciples. He doesn't want just ordinary average followers, He wants above average. When Jesus encounters the rich man, they have a conversation about life. They talk about the importance of following the commandments. Jesus finally tells him, "Okay buddy, if you want to be part of My team, if you want to follow Me, then give everything, not just part of you, but all of you, body, spirit, and mind." Jesus wants the man to give it all away so he can follow Jesus. Jesus raises the bar and the man looks at it and decides he'd rather be average, so he walks away.

Imagine how wonderful the Church and the world could be if we were all above average. Christians are called to make the world a better place, not just because it is something nice to say but because we are kingdom people and Jesus came proclaiming the kingdom. It is coming soon. St. Paul puts it another way, "Outdo one another in good works." Imagine if we could all outdo one another in good things? Imagine if we all could be more loving, more caring, and more generous? Imagine if each of us did one particular thing every day to make the world a better place? Now that is what I call above average. Why settle for anything less?

FOOD FOR THOUGHT

1. If we have low expectations for ourselves, we won't get far in life. Jesus raises the bar for us. He offers us the way to the Kingdom.

2. Discipleship is hard. Yet if we help each other, support each other, encourage each other, the road will be a little easier. Take some time and offer some encouragement or inspiration to your family or friends in their walk of faith.

3. Read: Matthew 10:1–16, Luke 5:1–10, Acts 9:1–19.

CHAPTER TWENTY FIVE

SWIMMING LIKE SALMON

*King Herod heard of it, for Jesus' name had be-
come known. Some were saying, "John the bap-
tizer has been raised from the dead; and for this
reason these powers are at work in him." But
others said, "It is Elijah." And others said, "It is
a prophet, like one of the prophets of old." But
when Herod heard of it, he said, "John, whom I
beheaded, has been raised."* (Mark 6:14–16)

One early Sunday morning at church, while I was
putting canned goods in our parish Loaves and
Fishes barrels, I noticed a case of tuna fish cans in the
bottom of the barrel which triggered some childhood
memories. At least once per week my mom made
tuna sandwiches for lunch. Of course, she made sure
that there were plenty of onions on it too. She liked
onions but I didn't. I tried to trade a sandwich with
my friend Paul. Paul always brought a baloney or sa-
lami sandwich. Paul didn't want to trade a yummy

baloney sandwich with mayo for a soggy onion-ridden tuna sandwich.

Once in a while mom made fish sticks for supper. These fish sticks hardly tasted like fish. I always had to douse them with extra ketchup so they'd taste better. When things were really good, my parents would go to Arthur Treacher's Fish and Chips restaurant. Everything was fried. I mean everything: fried flounder, fried shrimp, friend clam strips, and fried oysters. It wasn't until seminary that I had my first taste of real fish. It was 1997 and our seminary hosted a special luncheon in honor of a wealthy benefactor. The cook made salmon with a white wine and dill sauce reduction over wild rice and grilled vegetables. I had no idea what it was, but one of my friends leaned over and said, "Just try it, you'll like it." So I did and boy did I like it. I love poached salmon, grilled salmon, salmon kebabs, salmon cakes, salmon on a bagel, hot salmon and cold salmon.

But salmon have a tough life. They are born in the still streams and waters of the North Atlantic and North Pacific and slowly make their way downstream to the ocean. Then they have to avoid being eaten by sharks, whales, swordfish, or other large fish. God created them with a special brain that tells the salmon that they have to return to their birthplace, not just any river but the exact same river that they came from where they will lay their eggs. They have to swim in the ocean and find their way upstream. However, most fish swim downstream: trout, small and large mouth bass, carp, and catfish. And when trout see a lonely salmon fighting against the current, they yell, "Hey, you're going the wrong way!" It's so much easier swimming downstream. They just float along looking for flies or other bugs to eat. But those salmon are persistent fish. They swim upstream. Then they lay their eggs, and if they are strong enough, they make it back downstream and return back to the ocean, but most of them die in the process.

The prophets are a lot like salmon; they spend their whole life swimming upstream, against the ways of the world. God sent the prophets for one reason: Israel forgot about God. Can you imagine? Forgetting about God? I can. We forget God all the time. During the Christmas season, one of Jesus' names that we hear is Emmanuel, which is Hebrew for, "God with us." We cannot forget that God is with us. But Israel did. They got so distracted with so many things that God had to send special people like Amos, Hosea, Jonah, Habakkuk, Nahum, and others to remind Israel about God. Do you think they wanted to go and speak to those stiff-necked Israelites? No way! Amos was a Bedouin shepherd tending his sheep, having a good life, when God said, "Amos, you go and speak to the people of Israel." So Amos went. Same thing happened to Hosea. Hosea was a fig farmer, he made fig jam, fig jelly, fig wine, and then one day God came to Hosea and said "Okay Hosea, go to my people and preach." So Hosea went. God had the same conversation with Jonah, Jeremiah, Isaiah, and the others. God is stubborn.

The prophets reminded them about loving the poor, they reminded them about taking care of the sick and suffering, they reminded them about taking care of the widow, they reminded them that God was still alive and well and would come one day to judge them. One after the other the prophets were run out of town, stoned, or murdered. John the Baptist was beheaded; St. Stephen was stoned, and then St. Paul was beaten and put into prison. Why? Because Paul, just like the other prophets, reminded people about God.

Jesus, of course, is in the line of the prophets. It's hard though to be a prophet, it's hard to go against the stream, to stand up for what's right. Throughout Jesus' life we see him standing up to the Jewish leaders. He stood up to the rich, to the powerful, to the rulers; He stood up to Pilate and Herod. Jesus could not just go with the flow and be a follower. No, He was a man of God.

Our faith requires us to stand up for what is right even if it is not the most popular thing to do, and believe me, most of what is worth standing up for is not popular in the eyes of the world. Yet we have no other choice. We can be like those behemoth tunas floating around in the ocean, having an easy life, not having a care in the world, or we can be like those feisty salmon, going against the stream, showing the other fish in the world that there is another way to live life, that God is still with us.

FOOD FOR THOUGHT

1. I find it comforting to know that one of God's names is Emmanuel, "God with us." I find it comforting that in times of pain, in times of stress, in times of anguish and fear, God is always near. There are times when I feel so alone, yet when I stop for a moment, I remember that God is with me and I feel a lot better.

2. Salmon are not like other fish. They stand apart. They are like the prophets in the Old Testament. As disciples of Jesus, we too are supposed to stand out. We are supposed to be different from others, not *just* to be different, but to listen to the still small voice of God we must be different.

3. Read: Jonah 1:1–13, Isaiah 6:1–13, Mark 6:16–29.

RECOMMENDED READING

Enzo Bianchi. *Praying the Word: An Introduction to Lectio Divina*. Kalamazoo, MI: Cistercian Publications, 1998.

Raymond E. Brown. *Christ in the Gospels of the Liturgical Year (Expanded Edition with Essays)*. Collegeville, MN: The Liturgical Press, 2008.

James Martin. *Between Heaven and Mirth: Why Joy, Humor, and Laughter Are at the Heart of the Spiritual Life. New York,* NY: Harper One, 2011.

_____. *Becoming Who You Are*. Mahwah, NJ: Hidden Spring Books, 2006.

William C. Mills. *Encountering Jesus in the Gospels*. Rollinsford, NH: Orthodox Research Institute, 2012.

_____. *A 30 Day Retreat: A Personal Guide to Spiritual Renewal*. Mahwah, NJ: Paulist Press, 2010.

_____. *Our Father: A Prayer for Everyday Living*. Rollinsford, NH: Orthodox Research Institute, 2008.

Henry Nouwen. *Reading the Signs of Daily Life*. New York, NY: Harper One, 2013.

Barbara Brown Taylor. *An Altar in the World: A Geography of Faith*. New York, NY: Harper One, 2010.

ABOUT THE AUTHOR

Fr. William Mills, Ph.D., is the rector of the Nativity of the Holy Virgin Orthodox Church in Charlotte, North Carolina. Fr. Mills received his theological education at St. Vladimir's Seminary, in Crestwood, New York, and his doctorate in Pastoral Theology from the Union Institute and University in Cincinnati, Ohio. He is the author of numerous commentaries on the Gospel readings in the liturgical year as well as two books on pastoral ministry in the Orthodox Church. For more information about Fr. Mills, visit his website at www.williamcmills.com.

CPSIA information can be obtained
at www.ICGtesting.com
Printed in the USA
BVHW041304210921
617197BV00014B/335